62 HIKING TRAILS

NORTHERN OREGON CASCADES

BY DON & ROBERTA LOWE

The Touchstone Press
P.O. Box 81
Beaverton, Oregon 97005

ROAD NUMBER CONVERSION TABLE

The text and maps do not reflect the recent changes in the road numbers throughout the Mt. Hood National Forest. Most of the approaches are off highways or are well-marked by signs pointing to the trailheads. However, for those few exceptions the following conversion table should resolve confusion between the numbers that appear in the copy and the numbers you find on road signs along the drives to the trailheads.

Old Number	Current Number	Old Number	Current Number
FH (Road) 224	46	S-42	4220
		S-46A	380
N-13	13	S-53	4620
N-18	18	S-53C	210
N-20	670	S-57	57
(Trail Numbers 1 and 2)		S-58	58
		S-63	63
N-20	660	S-70	70
(Trail No. 3)		S-100	13
N-20	322	S-102	1340
(Trail No. 5)		S-160	16
N-100	1650	S-180P	650
N-118	1310	S-238	1828
N-119	640	S-238J	118
Road 19	1819	S-239	1825
Road 20E	200	S-239G	109
		S-338	4891
S-12	3512	S-338A	120
S-19	1810	S-339	4860
S-19A	1811	S-340	140
S-21	3550	S-344	10
S-25	1825	S-346	4890
(Trail Numbers 8, 29, 30, 31,32,33)		S-346A	220
		S-354	2639
S-25	100	S-356	3545
(The final 1.7 miles of driving for Trail Numbers 8, 32, 33)		S-386	3531
		S-389	522
		S-408	48
S-25D	382	S-409	200
S-27 (and 27)	207	S-456	240
S-30	3530	S-456A	250
S-32	2613	S-457	4610
S-32A	2632	S-458	2610
S-38	2618	S-505D	290
		S-708	6340
		S-739	6341
		S-806	4690
		S-820	6380
		S-829A	120
		10 Road	2612
		12 Road	2612
		20 Road	2620
		27 Road	2627

Maps Courtesy of
U.S. Geological Survey

INTRODUCTION

Nowhere in Oregon but the Portland metropolitan area do so many people have so many miles of prime hiking country practically in their backyards. A resident can rise at a reasonable hour, drive east to a trailhead, have a fine hike and return home with ample time to do something else that evening.

Oregonians have been enjoying the Mt. Hood area for more than a century. The first climbing group reached the summit of the peak in the 1850's; cycling to Government Camp enjoyed a burst of interest during the 1890's; skiing was introduced in the early 1900's and not long after that motoring through the quagmires or dust bowls of the Barlow Road became a favorite adventure. However, hiking was not especially popular until about 50 years ago. The Forest Service had been building trails as an aid in fire detection and surpression since just after the turn of the century and although the public was welcome to use them, not many people did. Paradise and Eden Parks were almost unknown in the early 1920's but by a decade later a use-path had been worn from Cloud Cap to Eden Park. In 1938 the Timberline Trail (No. 41) around Mt. Hood was completed, and interest has not waned since. The increased participation in hiking over the past decade has encouraged the construction of new routes and the reopening and regrading of many old fire trails that had long been abandoned.

The 62 hikes in this guide cover the majority of trails (except those in the Columbia Gorge accessible from I-80N) within the Mt. Hood National Forest, which extends along the Cascades from the Columbia River to just north of Mt. Jefferson. Trail No's. 1 through 3 are in the higher, southern part of the Columbia Gorge near Wahtum Lake, No's. 4 through 51 are near, or actually on, the slopes of Mt. Hood; No's. 52 through 54 are in the extensive Clackamas River drainage; No's. 55, 56 and 57 are in the Upper Collawash River drainage and the last five are in the Olallie Scenic Area just north of Mt. Jefferson.

All the trips are meritorious. But one area has more spectacular scenery than the others. That is the region along the Timberline Trail, particularly on the west, northwest and north sides of Mt. Hood. But every route has its special feature, from the exceptionally far-ranging views from the summits of many peaks, particularly those from Lookout Mountain (No. 18) and Olallie Butte (No. 60), the good swimming at Burnt (No. 31) or Wind (No. 43) Lakes or the scrumptuous huckleberries in the Zigzag (No. 30) and Tom Dick (No. 42) Mountains areas. At the very least, each hike provides an attractive place for enjoying the outdoors and that alone is enough justification for its inclusion in this guide.

Most trips in this book have at least two times when they are at their best. The timberline area on Mt. Hood is delightful in mid-summer when the snow-covered peak is as bright as the green grass and the dobs of color from the many wildflowers. By mid-September much of the snow has left the mountain, the lower slopes have turned golden but the hikes are no less attractive. The perkiness of the earlier season has only been replaced by the elegance and subdued beauty of fall's colors and textures. The climb to Bald Butte (No. 4) is another example of a trip so scenic at two seasons that you'll have to do it twice so you don't miss either. In late May the huge yellow blooms of balsamroot cover the summit area and the Upper Hood River Valley below is at its verdant best. But around the end of September the valley and the oaks and grassy slopes along the hike take on their fall colors and the trek is equally entrancing.

Except for those that boast especially good wildflower displays, the hikes through lower elevation woods don't change much throughout the summer and fall but they do take on different characteristics depending on the weather. Don't cancel an outing just because it's gloomy or raining. Some forests, the one along the first half of the Ramona Falls Loop (No. 32) for instance, are even more attractive in cloudy weather. Or make a hike after the first dusting of snow and you'll enjoy scenery similar to that shown on the cover of this guide.

Although a large percentage of the trails in the Mt. Hood National Forest (excluding the Columbia Gorge) are described in this guide, many places are left for you to discover on your own — for instance most of Surveyors Ridge near Mt. Hood's east slope and the Badger Creek drainage. If you're interested in finding routes not mentioned here or if you'd like more ideas for loops or possible car shuttles, refer to one of the three recreation maps prepared by the U.S. Forest Service. One map covers the entire Mt. Hood National Forest, another just the Mt. Hood Wilderness and the third is for the Columbia Gorge. They are available for $.50 each from the information center at the regional office, 319 S.W. Pine, Portland 97204, telephone 221-2877, the headquarters for the Mt. Hood National Forest, 2440 S.E. 195th (on Division Street if you're driving there), Portland 97233, telephone 667-0511 or from one of the district ranger stations. The U.S.G.S. topographic maps used in this guide are available from selected retail outlets, such as outdoor stores, or you can obtain them by sending $1.25 and identifying information (map name, state and scale) for each one to Branch of Distribution, Central Region, U.S. Geological Survey, Box 25286 Denver Federal Center, Denver, Colorado 80225.

Deer, bear, coyotes, cougars and smaller animals such as rabbits, racoons and porcupines live in the Mt. Hood National Forest but, unfortunately, the only mammals you'll probably see will be small rodents such as ground squirrels and chipmunks. If you travel alone your chances of spotting some wildlife are much better, of course. Ironically, conies, timid creatures not especially common in the Oregon Cascades, are dense on one scree slope on the popular trail to Mirror Lake (No. 42). Although you most likely won't be seeing many welcome wild animals, at least you won't be encountering many undesirable ones either, such as rattlesnakes. Ticks may be lurking on the bushes in the Clackamas River area and although you should be aware of their existence, you probably never will find one on your body or clothing. Mosquitoes are unwelcome companions on some trips during mid-summer, particularly in the lake country north of Mt. Jefferson, but repellent cream on exposed skin and spray on clothing minimizes their presence.

What you will see plenty of is wildflowers. Beginning with the anemones and avalanche lilies that start blooming even before the snow has completely melted from around them until the gentians of mid-fall, the alpine areas on Mt. Hood are brightened with wildflowers. Purple lupine, Indian paintbrush, ranging in colors from orange to bluish red to a dusty rose, white, bottle brush, pink and yellow monkey flowers on moist banks and marsh marigolds often actually growing in the streams are five of the most common varieties that thrive around timberline. The majority reach their peak around early August but this date varies considerably depending on the depth of the previous winter's snowpack and the temperature and rainfall during summer. A few years ago August was so cool and wet the wildflowers still were in good shape over the Labor Day weekend. Interestingly, the anemones (also known as western pasque flowers) that begin the season still are obvious in the fall but with a completely different guise. The low growing plants with white blooms change to foot high stalks that support seed pods with long, silky hairs, appropriately renamed old men of the mountains.

The trails below timberline have their own flower shows with rhododendrons and beargrass as the leading performers. Both bloom around the same time and frequently are seen together. Assorted other wildflowers thrive in the woods and particularly on open slopes. Probably the greatest variety in the Mt. Hood area graces the northwest slope of Chinidere Mountain (No. 2).

Douglas fir, lodgepole pine and cedar are the most common trees in the Mt. Hood National Forest but blending inconspicuously with them on the north and east slopes near Mt. Hood is another conifer. It's not too obvious until the end of October but then the needles of these western larch, also called tamaracks, turn a spectacular yellow-gold. You'll get the best view of their impressive presence from Polallie Ridge (No. 12).

Another plant that is unobtrusive until later in the season is the huckleberry. Around the end of August, though, the berries ripen and these bushes become wonderfully distracting. Although they grow along many of the trails, they are most abundant in the Zigzag Mountain (No. 30) region and the northwest side of Tom Dick Mountain (No. 42). Wild strawberries grow on the runs at Summit (see No. 40) and Multorpor-Ski Bowl (see No. 43) Ski Areas and wild blackberries are dense at the beginning of the Salmon Butte Trail (No. 25). As with any wild plant, be *sure* you know what you're eating. After the huckleberries are gone, the bushes turn vivid red and in open areas, such as those on Barlow Butte (No. 48), the slopes look like a giant rya rug.

Except for the 38-mile circuit around Mt. Hood on the Timberline Trail, all the trips in this guide can be accomplished in one day. As a matter of fact, because of the many lateral feeders, the Timberline Trail also can be done in several sessions of day hikes. However, if you want overnight trips you'll find many that will be suitable.

Self-issuing permits are required for both day hikers and backpackers in the Mt. Hood Wilderness. Registration boxes have been installed along all trails into the Wilderness so you don't have to go out of your way to fill one out. Elsewhere in the Mt. Hood National Forest, permits are not necessary for either hikers or backpackers.

Compared with most mountainous country, the Oregon Cascades are benign. Two potential, but infrequent, hazards are stream crossings and lightning. The former only are a problem on the fords of glacier fed streams along the Timberline Trail. Their volume decreases as the season progresses and the worst of them usually are bridged. The northern Oregon Cascades don't have daily lightning storms like the Colorado Rockies, for instance, but later in the summer they may occur. If a storm is building get off exposed ridges and high points and retreat into *dense* timber. Since accidents can happen on even the smoothest trail and mountain weather does change quickly, always include in your pack a wool hat, gloves, sweater, a windbreaker and a poncho or some other waterproof garment. A flashlight, first aid kit, whistle and extra food also should be standard equipment. A large umbrella is a good companion when the weather is "iffy" or you've deliberately gone out to see what a particular area looks like in the rain. It will keep your head, shoulders (and glasses, if you wear them) dry and you won't have to use those ponchos that trap your body heat while you're moving and get you as wet from the inside as you would from the inclement weather.

Although mention is made in the text if no water is available along the trail, you should always fill your bottle before leaving home or camp. Most people consider streams in the Mt. Hood National Forest that originate directly from snow melt or from drainage through the ground to be safe sources of drinking water. Water from lakes or outlets from lakes should be purified. Also, don't drink from streams fed by glacier melt as the rocky flour can irritate the lining of your intestines. The only places you have to worry about this is when you're on Mt. Hood at the Zigzag, Sandy and White Rivers, the Muddy Fork and Ladd, Coe, Eliot, Newton and Clark Creeks.

According to informal surveys made by U.S. Forest Service rangers, about half of the backpackers visiting the Mt. Hood Wilderness were doing so for the first time. Considering how long the increased interest in hiking and backpacking has been going on, this high number is surprising. For the benefit of these newcomers (and for others who may need a refresher course) a brief discussion about trail manners and the wilderness ethic follows.

Your main goal in the outdoors is to be as unobtrusive as possible, both to your fellow travelers and to nature.

Only a few people drop obvious litter such as candy and gum wrappers but many discard orange peels or egg shells since "they're organic and will decompose." Yes, they will but only after several unsightly years. If you see any of the above kinds of litter, pick it up and carry it out. Aural pollution, at least in the short run, is often worse than the visual variety. Be quiet. Don't shout, whistle, etc. Radios, tape players and CB units have no place in camp or on trails and as delightful as you feel your recorder or other musical instrument might be, others within its range probably would much prefer the natural sounds of a gurgling stream or the wind in the trees. Dogs are becoming an increasing problem. If yours is a barker or is aggressive toward people or other dogs, definitely leave it home. If your pooch is quiet and well-mannered at least *consider* not bringing it along.

Good trail manners also include not shortcutting switchbacks. On rocky slopes this can be dangerous to those below but on any terrain doing so establishes erosion channels that are ugly and expensive to repair.

Because backpackers have a greater impact, they have to be especially careful about behavior in the outdoors. Camp at least 100 feet from any stream or lake shore and away from meadows and grassy areas. The vegetation in these places can't tolerate the repeated compaction of tents and human feet. Disturb the area where you camp as little as possible. That is, cut no limbs, dig no trenches or hip holes, etc. Carry primus or similar type stoves. Wood fires scar the ground and make restoring an area even more difficult. Never wash yourself, your utensils or clothing or clean fish in a stream or lake and go well away from camp and water sources to bury (thoroughly) human wastes.

In other words, consider everything you do and attempt to have as little impact as possible. The old motto, "Take only pictures, Leave only footprints," is still a good one. (The one delightful exception is you can gobble huckleberries.)

All the hikes in this guide are on federal land managed by the U.S. Forest Service. If you have questions, suggestions, complaints or compliments about how the Mt. Hood Wilderness or the remaining portion of the Mt. Hood National Forest is being administered, write to the Mt. Hood National Forest. For information on conservation issues contact the Oregon Environmental Council, 2637 S.W. Water Avenue, Portland 97201, telephone 222-1963. If they're not directly involved in the particular issue that concerns you, they'll refer you to a group that is. Comments intended for the authors can be sent to them in care of The Touchstone Press, P.O. Box 81, Beaverton, Oregon 97005.

D.L.
R.L.

area map — shaded area covered by large maps, pages 10-11.

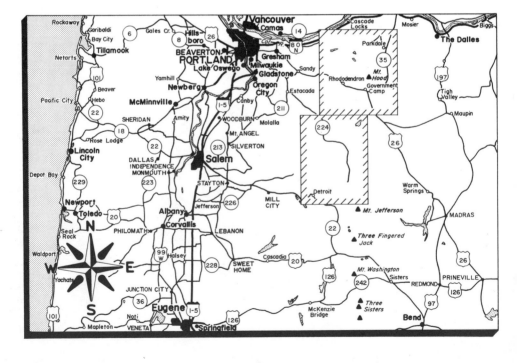

contents

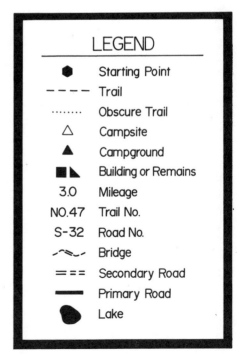

LEGEND

⬢	Starting Point
– – – –	Trail
....	Obscure Trail
△	Campsite
▲	Campground
■▶	Building or Remains
3.0	Mileage
NO.47	Trail No.
S-32	Road No.
⌒∾⌒	Bridge
= = =	Secondary Road
—	Primary Road
⬤	Lake

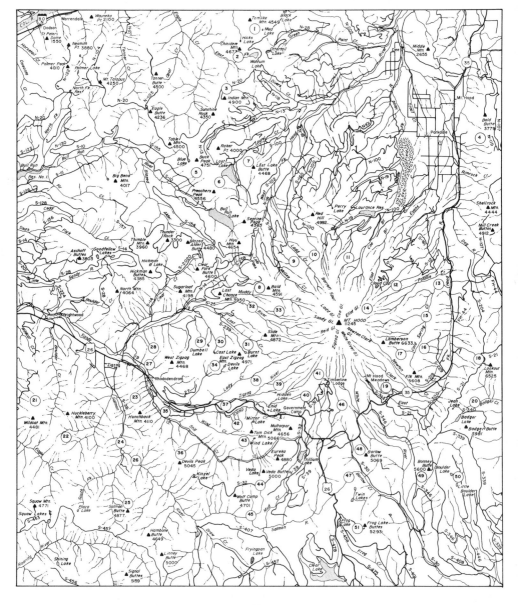

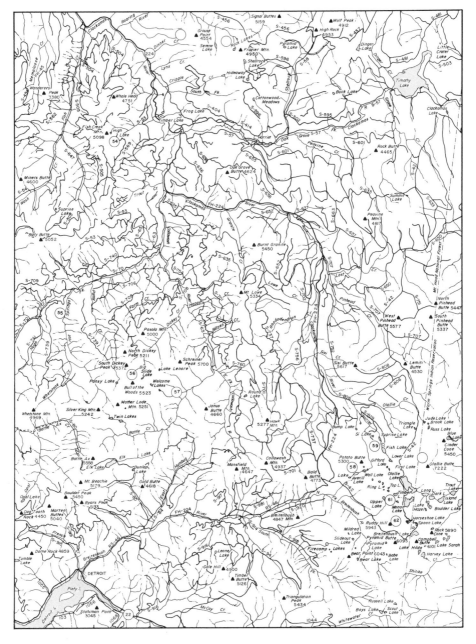

11

1 TOMLIKE MOUNTAIN

One day trip
Distance: 2.7 miles one way
Elevation gain: 880 feet; loss 350 feet
High point: 4,549 feet
Allow 1½ hours one way
Usually open late June through October
Topographic map:
  U.S.G.S. Bonneville Dam, Oreg.-Wash.
  15'   1957

The first three hikes in this guide begin above Wahtum Lake at the south edge of the Columbia Gorge and all climb to the summits of peaks that afford fine views. Mostly treeless Tomlike Mountain is the high point of massive Woolly Horn Ridge and from the top the view extends north to Mounts St. Helens, Rainier and Adams, west over much of the Gorge and south to Mt. Hood. You can approach the final mile along one of three routes. The most direct is to take the Anthill Trail No. 406B where there are indeed anthills. Or you can follow Road N-20 to Trails No. 406 or No. 406B. The longest way is along the first 1.8 miles of the hike to Chinidere Mountain (No. 2) then on a connector that meets Road N-20 south of Trail No. 406. Of course, you can combine two of these three into a loop. Carry water.

On US 26, drive 18 miles east of Sandy or 2.0 miles west of Rhododendron to the community of Zigzag and turn north on the Lolo Pass Road. This route is paved except for a 3.3 mile section on the north side of the pass. Twenty miles from US 26 come to the junction of Road S-100 to Lost Lake. Keep right, continuing on N-18, and 2.9 miles farther make an acute angle turn to the left onto Road N-13. A stop sign on

N-13 and a sign facing north stating *Wahtum Lake* identify the junction. Follow N-13 4.4 miles to a junction, keep right and travel uphill. Although this junction may not be signed, you're now on N-118. After 0.1 mile curve right and follow N-118, that is paved for a 2.0 mile section farther on, 4.6 miles to a junction. Curve left and go the final 1.0 mile to Road N-20 at the crest of a ridge above Wahtum Lake.

If you are approaching on Oregon 281 from Hood River go south 12 miles to the junction of the road to the plywood mill at Dee. Veer right, cross the Hood River then turn left and follow the signs pointing to Lost Lake 5.0 miles to the junction of N-13 and proceed as described above.

(Note: Road N-20 north from its junction with N-118 above Wahtum Lake is scheduled to be closed to vehicular traffic but, as of early 1979, this closure was not official so the road may be open as far as the gate, as indicated on the map.)

The Anthill Trail No. 406B begins between Road N-118 and N-20. Traverse north along the wooded slope then follow the crest, passing a good viewpoint. Descend to Road N-20, cross it and continue dropping for 0.4 mile to the junction of Trail No. 406 that heads back to Road N-20.

Keep right and walk gradually downhill for several yards to a sign on your left identifying the faint Tomlike Mountain Trail. Trail No. 406, the Herman Creek Trail, switchbacks just beyond here, and after passing the 0.3 mile spur to Mud Lake continues north 9.2 miles to the Columbia Gorge Work Center east of Cascade Locks.

If you plan to follow N-20, walk along it for 1.8 miles from its junction with N-118 to a sign stating *Herman Creek Trail No. 406.* Leave the road and walk on the level then begin descending gradually. During late June the white blooms of glacier lilies along this section are among the most dense in the Mt. Hood area.

At the junction just beyond No. 406B, the Anthill Trail, turn left onto the Tomlike Mountain Trail and hike along the crest through a forest of small evergreens. As you gradually climb to the north the trees become sparse and the trail increasingly faint. Come to a saddle at 2.1 miles and continue up the broad crest. Near the summit of the first rise above the saddle keep right where you come to a patch of low, very dense trees. Beyond this slight detour, continue up the rocky ridge top 0.5 mile to the summit.

Tomlike Mountain and Mt. Adams from Chinidere Mountain

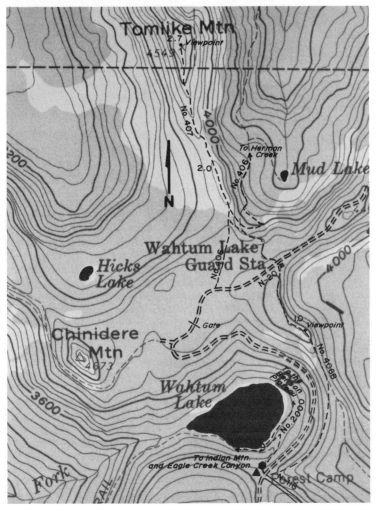

2 CHINIDERE MOUNTAIN

One day trip
Distance: 2 miles one way
Elevation gain: 975 feet; loss 200 feet
High point: 4,673 feet
Allow 1 hour one way
Usually open late June through October
Topographic map:
   U.S.G.S. Bonneville Dam, Oreg.-Wash.
   15'   1957

As with the hikes to nearby Tomlike (No. 1) and Indian (No. 3) Mountains, the view from the summit of Chinidere Mountain includes sightings of Mounts St. Helens, Rainier, Adams and Hood and the western portion of the Columbia Gorge. A special feature of this trip is the incredible variety of wildflowers along the southwest face of the peak during early July. You can extend the hike by descending along the Pacific Crest Trail No. 2000 for 1.5 miles north of Chinidere Mountain to a viewpoint or making a loop trip to Tomlike Mountain. You also could return along Road N-20 that involves no extra distance and saves 200 feet of uphill.

Proceed on US 26 18 miles east of Sandy or 2.0 miles west of Rhododendron to the community of Zigzag and turn north onto the Lolo Pass Road. This route is paved except for a 3.3 mile section on the north side of the pass. Twenty miles from US 26 come to the junction of Road S-100 to Lost Lake. Keep right, continuing on N-18, and 2.9 miles farther make an acute angle turn to the left onto Road N-13. A stop sign on N-13 and a sign facing north

stating *Wahtum Lake* identify the junction. Follow N-13 4.4 miles to a junction, keep right and travel uphill. Although this junction may not be signed, you're now on N-118. After 0.1 mile curve right and follow N-118, that is paved for a 2.0 mile section farther on, 4.6 miles to a junction. Curve left and go the final 1.0 mile to Road N-20 on the crest of a ridge above Wahtum Lake. A bulletin board off the west side of N-20 marks the beginning of the hike.

If you're approaching on Oregon 281 from Hood River go south 12 miles to the junction of the road to the plywood mill at Dee. Veer right, cross the Hood River then turn left and follow the signs pointing to Lost Lake 5.0 miles to the junction of N-13 and proceed as described above.

(Note: Road N-20 north from its junction with N-118 above Wahtum Lake is scheduled to be closed to vehicular traffic. However, as of early 1979 this closure was not official so the road may be open to the junction of Trail No. 445. If it is, you could shorten the hike to 0.7 mile one way by beginning there.)

Descend from the crest in one long switchback to the junction with the Pacific Crest Trail. Turn right and walk above the east side of the lake, crossing several wee streams. Beyond the lake, climb through woods and beargrass at an easy grade. Near 1.5 miles level off, cross a faint, unsigned old trail and resume climbing for a short distance to a junction. Trail No. 445 to the right contours 0.3 mile to Road N-20 and you'll be taking this path after you visit Chinidere Mountain if you plan to make the hike to Tomlike Mountain or loop back along N-20.

To reach Chinidere Mountain turn left after a few hundred feet, pass a large sign and 75 feet farther come to the Chinidere Mountain Trail on your right. Leave the Pacific Crest Trail and climb through woods in short switchbacks. Where the path forks just below the shale of the summit area, take the right fork and continue up along the rocky, open slope to the summit, the site of a former lookout as is obvious from the bits of rubble. Chinidere Mountain was named for the last ruling chief of the Wasco Indians.

If you saw wildflowers blooming along the spur to the summit, be sure to continue along the Pacific Crest Trail just a few hundred yards and cross the open southeast face. To visit the viewpoint continue gradually downhill along Trail No. 2000. Don't worry about missing the path to the overlook as the main trail makes its first switchback just 100 feet beyond it.

Indian Mountain from Chinidere Mountain

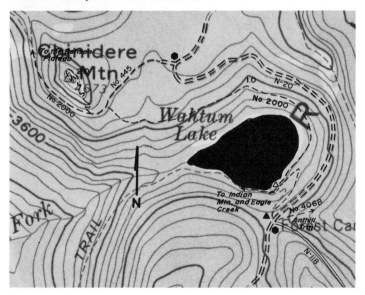

3 INDIAN MOUNTAIN

One day trip or backpack
Distance: 4.3 miles one way
Elevation gain: 1,400 feet; loss 250 feet
High point: 4,900 feet
Allow 2 hours one way
Usually open late June through October
Topographic map:
  U.S.G.S. Bonneville Dam, Oreg.-Wash.
  15'   1957

During the final mile of the climb of Indian Mountain you can look down over the wooded expanse of the upper Eagle Creek basin, one of the most remote areas of the Columbia Gorge. From the narrow, rocky summit the view includes the rugged north face of Mt. Hood and many landmarks in the Gorge, such as Tanner Butte just 3.5 miles to the northwest.

A scenic, interesting loop with uncommon views can be made by taking Trail No. 435 that descends to the north from Indian Springs Camp at 3.1 miles to the Eagle Creek Trail and following the latter up to your starting point at Wahtum Lake. This loop would add 3.0 miles and 1,200 feet of climbing. If instead you want to shorten the hike by 3.0 miles you can drive along N-20 to Indian Springs Camp.

On US 26, drive 18 miles east of Sandy or 2.0 miles west of Rhododendron to the community of Zigzag and turn north on the Lolo Pass Road. This route is paved except for a 3.3 mile section on the north side of the pass. Twenty miles from US 26 come to the junction of Road S-100 to Lost Lake. Keep right, continuing on N-18, and 2.9 miles farther make an acute angle turn to the left onto Road N-13. A stop sign on N-13 and a sign facing north stating *Wahtum*

Lake identify the junction. Follow N-13 4.4 miles to a junction, keep right and travel uphill. Although this junction may not be signed, you're now on N-118. After 0.1 mile curve right and follow N-118, that is paved for a 2.0 mile section farther on, 4.6 miles to a junction. Curve left and go the final 1.0 mile to Road N-20 at the crest of a ridge above Wahtum Lake. A bulletin board off the west side of N-20 marks the beginning of the hike.

If you are approaching from Hood River on Oregon 281, go south 12 miles to the junction of the road to the plywood mill at Dee. Veer right, cross the Hood River then turn left and follow the signs pointing to Lost Lake 5.0 miles to the junction of N-13 and proceed as described above.

Descend from the crest in one long switchback to the Pacific Crest Trail. The section to the right passes Chinidere Mountain (No. 2) after 1.8 miles. Turn left and travel along the south shore of Wahtum Lake. Near its west end come to the junction of Trail No. 440 that travels through Eagle Creek Gorge. You'll be returning along this route if you make the recommended loop. Turn left, staying on No. 2000, and traverse uphill along a wooded slope, occasionally crossing a few small, open rocky areas. Descend slightly then climb to near N-20. Walk parallel to and just below it then make a short set of switchbacks up a slope of large rocks where you can look south to Indian Mountain. Traverse through woods to a side road, cross to a sign listing several mileages and continue along the trail to Indian Springs Camp. Water can be obtained at its northwest edge.

Follow the trail that climbs from the south side of the camp and head toward the open ridge above to the southwest then curve right and traverse up the slope to the crest. Turn left here, leaving the Pacific Crest Trail that contours along the west side of Indian Mountain and continues south to Lolo Pass (see No. 5). Climb along the ridge top, cross N-20 and continue up the crest along an access road. Stay on the road where you pass an old metal sign at 4.2 miles and a short distance farther come to its end. Climb along a trail for 200 yards, switchbacking once, to the summit, the site of a former lookout cabin.

To make the loop, return to the stream at the northwest edge of Indian Springs Camp and descend steeply along Trail No. 435. Cross a scree slope, continue down through woods to Trail No. 440, turn right and climb 3.3 miles to Wahtum Lake.

Indian Mountain from Indian Springs Trail

4 BALD BUTTE

One day trip
Distance: 4 miles one way
Elevation gain: 2,180 feet; loss 260 feet
High point: 3,779 feet
Allow 2½ hours one way
Usually open mid-March through November
Topographic map:
  U.S.G.S. Hood River, Oreg.
  15'   1957

Bald Butte is one of the high points on the long ridge, called Hood River Mountain, that forms the eastern wall of the Lower and Upper Hood River Valleys. The panorama from its grassy summit is exquisite: a bird's eye view of the lush orchards and fields of the upper valley, the impressive horn-shaped east side of Mt. Hood, Mounts St. Helens and Rainier on the northern horizon and an especially attractive perspective of Mt. Adams. Carry water and also include extra clothing as the summit area often is very windy.

Proceed on Oregon 35 for 14.5 miles south of Hood River or 24 miles from its junction with US 26 to Smullen Road that heads east from the highway. This road is a short distance south of Toll Bridge Park and 0.1 mile north of a state highway maintenance station. Turn onto Smullen Road and after 0.4 mile where it curves right turn left onto a dirt road. After a short distance come to a flat area on your right and leave your car in this clearing unless you have a vehicle that can negotiate a rough and deeply-rutted bed.

Walk along the road for 0.4 mile, keeping right where a spur heads off to the left 0.2 mile from where you left your car. A sign on your left identifies the beginning of the Oak Ridge Trail No. 688A. Built in 1915, this route was one of the first trails in the Mt. Hood area but it was abandoned and not reopened until only a few years ago.

Turn left onto the trail and hike gradually uphill through an eclectic mixture of pine, oak, fir, alder and maple. Switchback right and soon have the first of many views of the Upper Hood River Valley and nearby Mt. Hood. The scene always is lovely but it's especially so around mid-October when the valley takes on the muted hues of fall color. Wind upward along slopes covered with grass and scattered oaks. Caution: watch for a few sections of poison oak along the trail. After about a dozen switchbacks you'll be able to see your destination, the mostly grassy highpoint to the northeast, and a little farther you'll have your first views of Mounts St. Helens, Adams and Rainier. Switchback a few more times through the grass then enter woods of Douglas fir and delicate ground cover. Cross a clearing that affords another good view and reenter woods. Traverse across the top of an old clearcut, make several switchbacks and come to Road N-119. The trail that continues across the road follows Surveyors Ridge south for several miles.

Turn left and walk along the road for 150 yards to a sign on your left identifyingTrail No. 688, the Surveyors Ridge Trail. Follow it on the level through a clearcut, passing another viewpoint, enter woods and begin descending, losing 250 feet of elevation in 0.5 mile. Come to the treeless corridor accompanying the four sets of power lines and follow the road that goes under them.

Curve left on the road and climb to the base of a tower. Continue north up along the road, travel on the level through woods, drop slightly and make the final climb along the open slope to the summit. During late spring these slopes are a yellow swath of balsamroot blooms. Until just a few years ago a tall lookout tower stood on the crest. The summit area is a popular launching site for hang gliders so you may have some entertainment while you enjoy your lunch and the view. Mt. Defiance, the highest point in the Columbia Gorge, is the peak with the slim microwave tower to the northwest.

Mt. Hood from Bald Butte

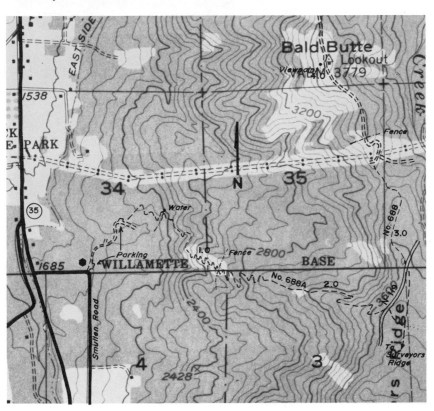

19

5 BUCK PEAK

One day trip
Distance: 7.5 miles one way
Elevation gain: 1,550 feet; loss 200 feet
High point: 4,751 feet
Allow 4 to 5 hours one way
Usually open late June through October
Topographic map:
   U.S.G.S. Bull Run Lake, Oreg.
   7.5'   1962

The climb to Buck Peak begins at Lolo Pass and follows the Pacific Crest Trail north for all but the last 0.1 mile. From the summit you'll have fine views of the northwest side of Mt. Hood and the southern portion of the Columbia Gorge. Carry water.

By establishing a long car shuttle, you can make a scenic 25 mile one-way backpack past Indian Mountain and through the Columbia Gorge to I-80N. The first satisfactory place for a camp is Indian Springs at 13.0 miles (No. 3). From there you can reach the freeway by following the Eagle Creek Trail (again, see No. 3) to the Eagle Creek Fish Hatchery at Exit 41, the Herman Creek Trail (see No. 1) or the Pacific Crest Trail across the Benson Plateau (see No. 2). The latter two end at the Columbia Gorge Work Center east of Cascade Locks.

On US 26, drive 18 miles east of Sandy or 2.0 miles west of Rhododendron to the community of Zigzag and turn north on the Lolo Pass Road. Ten miles from the highway come to Lolo Pass where a sign on the left (north) side of the road identifies the beginning of the hike. Parking is available here and several yards farther along the opposite shoulder where the section of the Pacific Crest Trail to the south begins.

Walk on the level for a few hundred feet, climb through a cleared area under the transmission lines and begin traversing north at a moderate uphill grade. Mt. Hood looms across the valley to the east. If you return late in the day and the atmospheric conditions are right, you'll enjoy a beautiful alpineglow on the peak. Farther on, a sheer cliff face above the trail and appropriately located trees make a photogenic frame for Mt. Adams.

Near 0.9 mile cross a scree slope and resume traveling in woods. Walk almost on the level along a bench then drop slightly and wind across a saddle. Traverse the east and north sides of Sentinel Peak. Cross a small open area then again descend briefly. Reenter woods and at 4.0 miles come to an old fire break and follow it for 0.1 mile to a saddle and the junction of the Huckleberry Trail No. 617 that descends for 1.7 miles to the southwest tip of Lost Lake (No. 6). (This connector is scheduled to be closed in 1980.)

Keep straight (left) on the Pacific Crest Trail, reenter woods and resume climbing. Pass a sign identifying Salvation Springs Camp, switchback up a few times between Preachers Peak and Devils Pulpit then continue traversing the northeast facing side of the ridge. Eventually, you have a good view down onto Lost Lake. Near 5.8 miles the route travels along a broad, level ridge crest for 0.4 mile then returns to traversing. At 6.2 miles, where the trail curves sharply left, you'll have the first view of the summit of Buck Peak.

Descend gradually for 0.5 mile then resume the moderate uphill grade. Cross to the west side of the slope and 250 feet farther come to a sign identifying the junction of the spur to Buck Peak. Keep right and wind up for 0.1 mile to the large summit area, the site of a former lookout cabin.

If you're backpacking to the Columbia River, continue north on the Pacific Crest Trail. Descend in a series of switchbacks then traverse at a reasonable uphill grade for 3.5 miles. Walk near Road N-20 for a short distance, cross it and travel along the open west slope of Indian Mountain. One mile from N-20 curve right, cross over the crest and drop 0.4 mile to Indian Springs Camp.

Buck Peak and Blue Lake

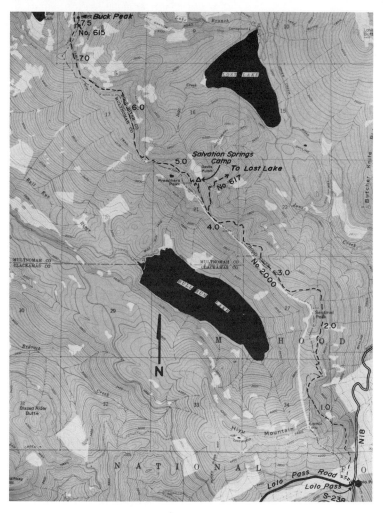

6 LOST LAKE TRAIL

One-half day trip
Distance: 3 miles round trip
Elevation gain: 100 feet
High point: 3,190 feet
Allow 1½ hours round trip
Usually open June through November
Topographic map:
  U.S.G.S. Bull Run Lake, Oreg.
  7.5'   1962

The almost level Lost Lake Trail circles the lake, often traveling only inches from the water's edge. During the first part of the hike the firs and low bushes perfectly frame Mt. Hood and this section is popular with photographers. Early in the season or after a period of rain, the trail may be swampy in a few places. If you want a longer day of hiking you could combine this loop with the climb to the summit of Lost Lake Butte (No. 7) that rises above the east shore.

Proceed on US 26 18 miles east of Sandy or 2.0 miles west of Rhododendron to the community of Zigzag and turn north onto the Lolo Pass Road. This route is paved except for a 3.3 mile section on the north side of the pass. Twenty miles from US 26 come to the junction of Road S-100 and keep left on it as indicated by the sign stating *Lost Lake 7*. Continue on S-100 to near the northeastern end of the lake then follow the signs pointing right to Store and Campground. From the small store and the cluster of buildings at the northern tip of the lake drive west, crossing the outlet creek, and continue 0.2 mile beyond the buildings to the large turnaround at the road's end where a sign stating *Lake Shore Trail* marks the beginning of the hike.

If you're approaching from the Hood River area, go south on Oregon 281 for 12 miles to the junction of the road to the plywood mill at Dee. Veer right, leaving the highway, cross the Hood River then turn left and follow signs to Lost Lake for 5.0 miles to the junction of N-13 to Wahtum Lake. Keep left on the Lolo Pass Road, which is eventually numbered N-18, 3.0 miles to the junction of S-100, turn right and continue the 7.0 miles to the lake as described above.

Walk on the level through attractive woods for 0.7 mile to a more open area at several inlet creeks. Boardwalks have been constructed along this swamp-like stretch so crossing the delta presents no problems. Resume traveling through woods and near 0.9 mile, where the trail is about 200 feet from the lake, pass a dry campsite between the trail and the shore that is a good place for a snack stop before finishing the hike.

Soon begin walking very near the shore and traverse a small scree slope before continuing beside the water's edge. (By the way, Lost Lake is the deepest in the Mt. Hood National Forest.) Gain and lose some minor amounts of elevation then at the south end of the lake come to the junction of the Huckleberry Trail No. 617 that climbs for 1.7 miles to the Pacific Crest Trail and the route to Buck Peak (No. 5). (This connector is scheduled to be closed in 1980.)

Keep left and farther on pass below some rustic buildings then continue along the trail for 0.7 mile to where it meets a road. Hike north on the road closest to the shore for 0.5 mile to reach your starting point.

22

Fishermen on Lost Lake

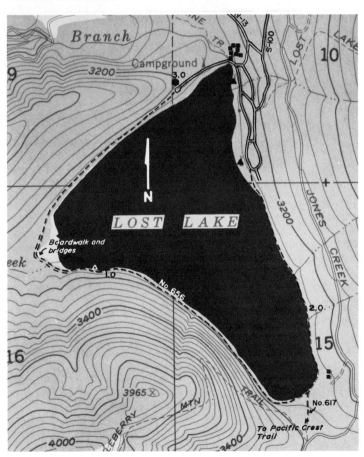

7 LOST LAKE BUTTE

One-half day trip
Distance: 2 miles one way
Elevation gain: 1,270 feet
High point: 4,468 feet
Allow 1 to 1½ hours one way
Usually open June through October
Topographic map:
  U.S.G.S. Bull Run Lake, Oreg.
  7.5'   1962

From the summit of Lost Lake Butte, which rises straightaway from the east shore of Lost Lake, you'll be able to see Mounts Hood, Jefferson, St. Helens and Adams in addition to such lesser peaks as Mt. Defiance and Larch and Indian (No. 3) Mountains in the Columbia Gorge, tower-topped Hickman Butte to the south and the Upper Hood River Valley. Since the trailheads for the short trips to Lost Lake Butte and around Lost Lake (No. 6) are close, combining the two is convenient if you want a longer day of hiking. Carry water as none is available along the climb.

Drive on US 26 18 miles east of Sandy or 2.0 miles west of Rhododendron to the community of Zigzag and turn north onto the Lolo Pass Road. This route is paved except for a 3.3 mile section on the north side of the pass. Twenty miles from US 26 come to the junction of Road S-100 and keep left on it as indicated by the sign stating *Lost Lake 7*. Continue on S-100 to near the northeastern end of the lake then keep left (east) at roads going west to the campground and shore and continue on S-102 to a sign on the right (west) shoulder pointing across the road to the beginning of the Lost Lake Butte Trail. Ample parking spaces are available along the sides of the road.

If you're approaching from the Hood River area go south on Oregon 281 for 12 miles to the junction of the road to the plywood mill at Dee. Veer right, leaving the highway, cross the Hood River then turn left and follow signs to Lost Lake for 5.0 miles to the junction of N-13 to Wahtum Lake. Keep left on the Lolo Pass Road that eventually is numbered N-18, 3.0 miles to the junction of S-100, turn right and continue the 7.0 miles to the lake as described above.

The trail begins on the east side of the road and follows a gradual uphill grade through deep woods for a short distance before beginning to rise at a more noticeable angle. Near 0.8 mile rhododendron bushes become plentiful and as the trail gains elevation the trees become smaller and the other vegetation less dense. During the final 0.8 mile to the summit the route makes several switchbacks of uneven length. You'll have your first views of Lost Lake and Mounts St. Helens and Adams before you reach the top, the site of a former lookout cabin.

Lost Lake Butte from Lost Lake

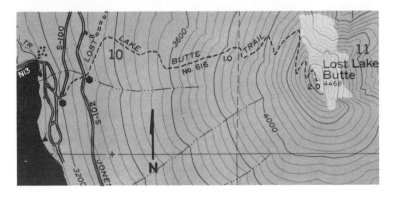

8 BALD MOUNTAIN

One day trip
Distance: 3.9 miles one way
Elevation gain: 1,860 feet
High point: 4,591 feet
Allow 2 hours one way
Usually open June through October
Topographic map:
   U.S.G.S. Bull Run, Oreg.
   7.5'   1962

Even though you know it's going to be there, the sudden appearance of the west face of Mt. Hood, only 4.0 miles from the summit of Bald Mountain, is a wonderful surprise. Most of the hike is along a former section of the Timberline Trail and you can take advantage of the network of trails resulting from the realignment by doing the trip as one of two loops. The easier, which adds a total of 4.0 miles and 50 feet of elevation gain, follows the route of the Ramona Falls Loop (No. 32). The other, harder with 5.0 miles and 400 feet of uphill, follows the Pacific Crest Trail No. 2000 from Bald Mountain to the Ramona Falls Loop. This longer circuit in-volves a ford of the Muddy Fork that is a problem only during times of freshet. (See the third subsection of No. 41 for a description of this route.)

Proceed on US 26 18 miles east of Sandy or 2.0 miles west of Rhododendron to the community of Zigzag and turn north on the Lolo Pass Road. Drive 4.1 miles to a sign marking the road to McNeil Campground and Ramona Falls and turn right. Go downhill 0.6 mile, turn right, cross a bridge and pass the entrance to McNeil Campground. Follow S-25 for 1.5 miles, keep straight (left) then continue on now unpaved S-25 the final 1.7 miles to the large parking area at the end of the road. The trail begins from the northeast edge of the loop.

Walk several yards across the rocky high water area to a tall bridge over the Sandy River. At the north end of the span turn right and climb a couple hundred feet to a junction. Keep straight (left) as indicated by the sign stating *Bald Mountain Trail ½*. Soon cross Ramona Creek and continue on the level.

Where the trail curves sharply right veer left into a camping area where small wooden signs state *Bald Mountain Trail No. 784* and *Bald Mountain 3*. Walk west several yards to the edge of the bank and cross the Muddy Fork on a log bridge. Turn left and climb through dense brush for a short distance then enter woods of trees considerably larger than the lodgepole pines seen earlier. Traverse up at a steady, moderate grade along the smooth, spongy trail. Near 1.7 miles make two switchbacks.

Cross a wee scree slope, just beyond it hop a small stream, the last source of water, then make five switchbacks. Go over the face of the crest and continue up to the junction of the Timberline and Pacific Crest Trails.

Turn right onto the Pacific Crest Trail, following the sign pointing to Ramona Falls, and 150 yards from the four-way junction watch for an unsigned path on your left. Veer left onto the path, travel parallel to the main route for several yards then curve left and begin climbing. Rise more steeply several hundred feet before the top and 0.4 mile from the Pacific Crest Trail come to the flat summit. Walk to the east edge of the bushes for the best view. Cast (No. 29) and East Zigzag (No. 31) Mountains are to the south, Yocum Ridge (No. 33) forms the south wall of the Muddy Fork valley and Barrett Spur (No. 10) is the subsidiary peak on the northwest shoulder of Mt. Hood. McNeil shelter (No. 9) is barely discernible to the east and a section of No. 2000 is visible directly below you.

Mt. Hood from the summit of Bald Mountain

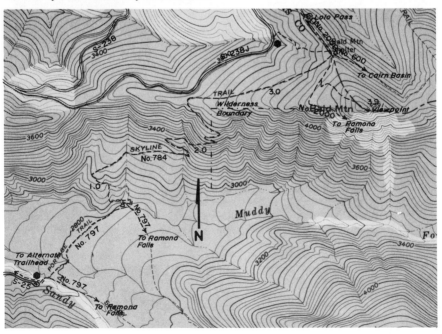

9 CATHEDRAL RIDGE TO McNEIL POINT

One day trip
Distance: 4 miles one way
Elevation gain: 2,850 feet; loss 200 feet
High point: 6,240 feet
Allow 3 hours one way
Usually open July through October
Topographic maps:
   U.S.G.S. Bull Run Lake, Oreg.
   7.5'   1962
   U.S.G.S. Cathedral Ridge, Oreg.
   7.5'   1962

Like the spokes around a hub, many routes afford access to the spectacularly scenic Timberline Trail (No. 41) around Mt. Hood: No's. 8 through 12, 17, 32, 33, 34, 38, 39, 40 and 46. The sometimes steep Cathedral Ridge Trail meets the Timberline Trail in a grassy swale and from there you can head north the short distance to Cairn Basin and Eden Park or continue up to the fine viewpoint at McNeil shelter. A steep path winds directly down from the stone cabin to the Timberline Trail so you could make a little loop on your return (see the Ramona Falls to Cairn Basin subsection of No. 41). No water is available until 3.0 miles.

Drive on US 26 18 miles east of Sandy or 2.0 miles west of Rhododendron to the community of Zigzag and turn north on the Lolo Pass Road. Proceed 10 miles to the pass then go downhill on the Lolo Pass Road along a section that is unpaved and rough 3.3 miles to the junction of paved Road S-19. Turn sharply right and after 1.7 miles turn up to the left onto unpaved Road S-19A. Continue the final 2.6 miles to a clearcut where a sign on your left identifies the trailhead.

Climb 150 feet along a cat road then veer left onto a trail as indicated by a sign stating *Hikers.* Rise very steeply to the crest, turn left and continue up to the top of the clearcut. Enter woods sprinkled with rhododendron bushes and continue climbing, sometimes at a very steep grade, in 13 switchbacks to the crest of the ridge. Travel at a considerably more moderate grade near the edge then enter an area of small trees and rise more noticeably.

Resume walking in woods of larger trees then go through a corridor-like meadow that affords a good view of Mt. Hood and is dense with beargrass. At the far end of the clearing resume climbing then begin traversing the west side of a steep slope. At 2.8 miles, and near timberline, come to the lower end of a swale. Pass a small boulder field and hike up the little valley of grass and heather, passing above a long tarn that dries up later in the summer then cross a small stream and come to the junction of the Timberline Trail.

To reach McNeil Point turn left on the Timberline Trail and walk 100 feet to the stream you crossed just below the junction. Turn right, leaving No. 600, and follow a path up the lovely swale. Assorted wildflowers brighten this area through the entire season. Aim for the head of the valley and climb steeply cross-country for the final 500 linear feet to a well-worn use-trail running perpendicular to the valley.

Turn right onto the path, cross a scree slope, go over a low crest and descend slightly then curve left. The tread is faint here for several yards but you can see the obvious route traversing the slope ahead. Cross a good-sized stream, the last source of water, and pass more wildflowers such as cassiope (white heather), not an especially common flower in the Mt. Hood area. Continue traversing and just beyond a rocky stretch come to a crest. Veer right here and follow a path several hundred feet gradually downhill to the shelter.

Mt. Hood's west face fills the view to the east, the deep canyon of the Muddy Fork is directly below and Yocum Ridge (No. 33) forms the massive valley's south wall. No. 2000, the Pacific Crest Trail, is obvious as it crosses Bald Mountain (No. 8) and you can follow most of the route of the possible loop back along the Timberline Trail. Hickman Butte is the flat-topped peak with the lookout tower and Larch Mountain in the Columbia Gorge, Lost Lake (No. 6), Salmon Butte (No. 25) and Wildcat (No. 21) and East Zigzag (No. 31) Mountains are a few of the many other visible landmarks.

McNeil Shelter

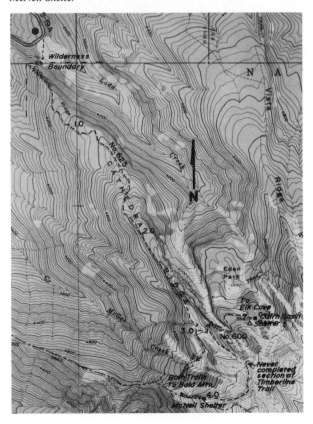

10 VISTA RIDGE and BARRETT SPUR

One day trip or backpack
Distance: 4.3 miles one way
Elevation gain: 3,480 feet
High point: 7,850 feet
Allow 3 to 3½ hours one way
Usually open late July through mid-October
Topographic map:
    U.S.G.S. Cathedral Ridge, Oreg.
    7.5'   1962

Barrett Spur is the prominent bulge on the lower northwestern flank of Mt. Hood and from the summit of this immense, rocky ridge you'll have a close-up look down onto Coe and Ladd Glaciers and far-ranging views to the north and west. The final 1.3 miles of the hike is cross-country but if you'd prefer a shorter, easier trailless trip, you could climb to a grassy viewpoint to the west. You also could make a loop (along trails) through Cairn Basin and Eden Park that would add 1.8 miles and 450 feet of uphill.

Proceed on US 26 18 miles east of Sandy or 2.0 miles west of Rhododendron to the community of Zigzag and turn north on the Lolo Pass Road. Ten miles from the highway come to Lolo Pass and continue downhill along the Lolo Pass Road 6.4 miles to the junction on your right of S-160. (The surface is unpaved and rough for 3.3 miles beyond the pass.) Turn right, as indicated by the sign pointing to Vista Ridge Trail, after 0.8 mile turn left and 3.8 miles farther curve left, still on S-160. After 0.7 mile turn right onto unpaved N-100. Drive 3.5 miles, keeping on N-100 at several side spurs, to the end of the passable road where a sign marks the beginning of the Vista Ridge Trail. The road is very rough for the final 0.5 mile.

If you are approaching from the Hood River area proceed south on Oregon 281 or 35 to the west end of Parkdale then go west on Baseline Road for 1.0 mile to a junction and keep left, following the sign to Red Hill. After 0.2 mile keep straight (right) at the junction of N-19 then a short distance farther keep left on N-100 and follow it 17.8 miles to the trailhead.

Walk along an old road for 200 yards then begin traveling on a trail and enter woods. Hike on the level 0.5 mile to the junction of the trail to Red Hill Guard Station. Bear right and traverse then curve into a small ravine. Make a set of switchbacks and continue up through woods at a moderate to gradual grade.

Switchback at 1.9 miles and 0.2 mile farther, as the trees start to thin, begin climbing more noticeably. Near timberline come to the junction of the trail to Eden Park, the northern leg of the possible loop. To go directly to Barrett Spur stay left on No. 626 and traverse 0.2 mile along an open slope to Wy'east Basin and the junction of the Timberline Trail. (See the Cairn Basin to Elk Cove subsection of No. 41.) Water is available from a stream a short distance to the east along the Timberline Trail.

To reach the summit of Barrett Spur leave the Timberline Trail at Wy'east Basin and climb cross-country to the southeast. Turn around frequently and study the terrain so on the descent you'll be able to locate where you left the trail. After about 0.5 mile reach the crest of the lower portion of the spur. Climb along the crest and after another 0.5 mile come to a broad saddle below the rocky summit block. Although the grade increases considerably beyond here, the footing is good. Come to the summit ridge and continue to another high point then descend slightly, being careful not to go near the edge of any of the steep snow slopes. Resume climbing and scramble over boulders for 0.1 mile to a broad, level area that is a good stopping place.

To make the shorter and easier of the cross-country trips, follow the Timberline Trail west from Wy'east Basin toward Cairn Basin. Go around the face of a ridge and about 0.5 mile from the junction look for a grassy swath and follow it up 0.9 mile to a good viewpoint on a nubbin just below the grassline.

30

Hikers below Barrett Spur

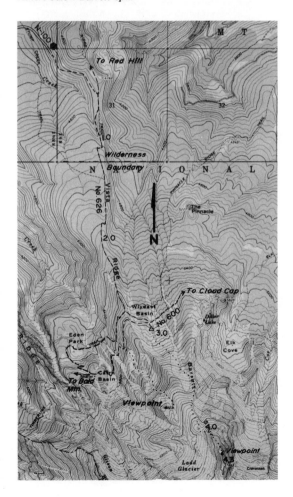

11 ELK COVE TRAIL

One day trip or backpack
Distance: 3.3 miles one way
Elevation gain: 1,800 feet
High point: 5,450 feet
Allow 2 hours one way
Usually open July through October
Topographic map:
  U.S.G.S. Cathedral Ridge, Oreg.
  7.5'   1962

Elk Cove is the most northerly and rugged of the several exceptionally scenic basins situated at timberline on the northern and northwestern slopes of Mt. Hood. Since the Timberline Trail passes through the cove, you can follow it east or west through more spectacular terrain (see the Cairn Basin to Elk Cove and Elk Cove to Cloud Cap subsections of No. 41). A more strenuous side trip would be the climb of Barrett Spur (No. 10), the rocky ridge directly above Elk Cove to the south that separates Coe and Ladd Glaciers.

Drive on Oregon 35 for 15.5 miles from its junction with US 26 or 23.5 miles south of Hood River to a sign stating *Cooper Spur* and *Tilly Jane Campground* and turn west. After 2.3 miles keep straight (right). Five miles farther turn left, following the sign pointing to Laurence Lake and after 0.5 mile again turn left as indicated by a sign. Two and one-half miles farther keep right then continue 1.2 miles to a junction just before the dam at Laurence Lake and keep straight. Six-tenths mile more, beyond the lake, turn left at a sign pointing to Trail No. 630. Keep left after 1.0 mile, this time following the sign indicating the direction to Trail No. 631, and drive the final 1.3 miles to a sign that marks the beginning of the Elk Cove Trail. Limited parking space is available along the side of the road.

From the Hood River area you also can proceed south on Oregon 281 or 35 to the west end of the town of Parkdale then head south 3.0 miles to a sign pointing right (west) to Laurence Lake. Turn right and continue to the trailhead as described above.

Traverse up the bank for several yards then curve right and continue uphill along the wooded slope. Make two very short switchbacks and hike along the ridge crest. Periodically, you'll have views of Mt. Hood. Travel above a logged area and reenter woods at the junction of the old Elk Cove Trail. Keep right on the main route and climb at a slightly steeper grade along the crest. Come to a good view of Mt. Hood and descend through a more open area. Pass the sign marking the wilderness boundary then regain the elevation you just lost and reenter woods.

Where you pass a low rocky crest to your left a few feet above the trail, leave the main route and climb to the overlook for a view down into Coe Creek gorge. Descend briefly then resume climbing. The grade is considerably steeper for a short distance but then resumes its usual moderate angle. As the elevation increases the woods gradually become composed of larger conifers. Walk almost on the level past dense patches of avalanche lilies that reach their blooming peak during mid-July.

Make an easy ford of a wide, shallow stream and continue up through attractive woods past more clusters of the white lilies. The trail climbs a ravine in several short, loose switchbacks then is straight for 0.1 mile until it meets the Timberline Trail at the edge of Elk Cove. Turn right and walk 100 yards to the stream that flows through the center of the basin and is a fine place for a lunch stop. If you're doing the trip as a backpack DO NOT CAMP in the meadows. Instead, pitch your tent in the woods just to the north of the junction of the Timberline and Elk Cove Trails.

Mt. Hood from the viewpoint

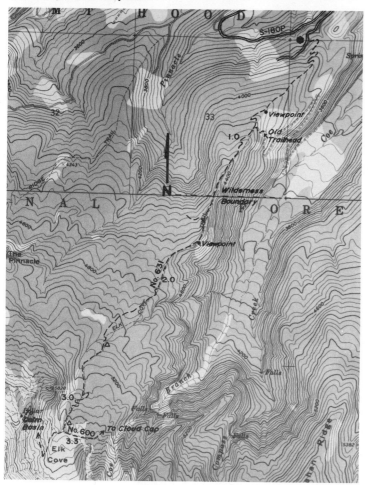

12 TILLY JANE TRAIL

One day trip or backpack
Distance: 3.2 miles one way
Elevation gain: 2,160 feet
High point: 5,940 feet
Allow 2½ hours one way
Usually open mid-June through October
Topographic maps:
  U.S.G.S. Cathedral Ridge, Oreg.
  7.5'   1962
  U.S.G.S. Dog River, Oreg.
  7.5'   1962

Like the Alpine Trail (No. 40), the Tilly Jane Trail from Cooper Ski Area to Cloud Cap doubles as a ski trail during the winter. In 1979 Forest Service crews are scheduled to brush out the old Polallie Ridge Trail No. 643A that follows the crest of the ridge just to the south of the one taken by the Tilly Jane Trail. When this work is completed you'll be able to make a fun loop that involves a negligible amount of extra uphill and distance. Also, a little loop is possible along the Timberline Trail at the high end of the hike but it would add 800 feet of climbing and 1.5 miles. Since the hike ends at Road S-12, you could do the trip one way by establishing a car shuttle (see No. 14). Water is not available until 2.7 miles.

Proceed on Oregon 35 for 15.5 miles from its junction with US 26 or 23.5 miles south of Hood River to a sign stating *Cooper Spur* and *Tilly Jane Campground* and turn west. After 2.3 miles turn left onto Road S-12 and follow it 1.0 mile to the beginning of the one-way loop to Cooper Spur Ski Area.

If you plan to take the Polallie Ridge Trail up, keep left and proceed 0.6 mile to the parking turnouts at the bottom of the ski area. Hike up the slope, cross a road and continue uphill to the upper terminus of the poma lift. You can see Mounts Adams and Rainier and the Upper Hood River Valley and Bald Butte (No. 4) and if you make the trip during late October you'll be impressed, and perhaps surprised, by the profusion of golden-yellow larch trees on the surrounding slopes. At the top of the lift turn right onto a road, and after several yards, keep left and walk along the crest. Eventually, you'll have views down into the immense, rugged canyon holding Polallie Creek. About 2.0 miles from the lift walk on the level then descend briefly. Resume climbing and travel through deeper woods to the junction with Trail No. 600A just south of the former cookhouse.

If you plan to follow the Tilly Jane Trail No. 643 up, keep right at the one-way loop to Cooper Spur Ski Area and continue along S-12. After 0.4 mile pass the exit end of the loop and 200 feet farther come to a sign on your left identifying the beginning of the trail.

Walk up a wide swath then traverse through woods to the junction at 0.7 mile of the trail to the ski area. Keep right and continue uphill. Enter the beargrass zone and at 1.6 miles come to the top of a ridge where you'll have a view of Mt. Hood. Curve right and climb along the crest.

Leave the crest and traverse along the north facing slope where you'll have glimpses down onto the Hood River Valley and north to Mounts St. Helens, Rainier and Adams. Enter deep woods of large trees and pass Tilly Jane Shelter that is left open during the winter. Pass a second building that once served as a cookhouse and just west of it turn left onto Trail No. 600A. After about 100 feet come to the junction of the route that goes to Cloud Cap Saddle Campground.

Turn right; after a short distance go in and out of a small canyon, travel above Tilly Jane Campground and climb the final 0.6 mile to the junction with the Timberline Trail No. 600 at the south end of Cloud Cap Saddle Campground. To visit charming Cloud Cap Inn, walk north through the campground to Road S-12 and follow it up 0.2 mile to the turnaround.

To make the high loop, head south along the Timberline Trail 1.0 mile to the junction of No. 600A. (Refer to the Cloud Cap to Elk Meadows subsection of No. 41.) Turn left and descend 1.0 mile to the junction with No. 643 near the cookhouse.

Trail crew workers at Tilly Jane

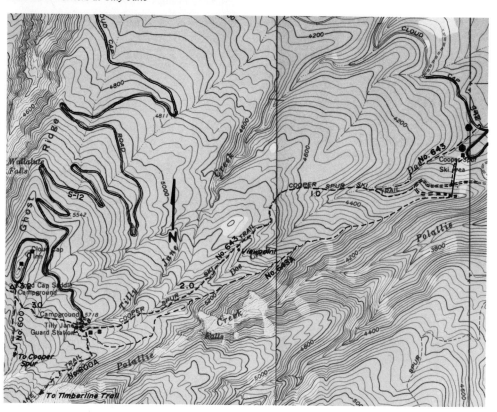

13 TAMANAWAS FALLS

One-half day trip
Distance: 1.6 miles one way
Elevation gain: 440 feet
High point: 3,490 feet
Allow 1 hour one way
Usually open late April through November
Topographic map:
  U.S.G.S. Dog River, Oreg.
  7.5'   1962

The easy trail to Tamanawas Falls traverses a narrow, wooded canyon beside rambunctious Cold Spring Creek before reaching the viewpoint near the base of the 100 foot high cascade. The hike is a good choice for a short, leisurely trip and several spots along the stream afford attractive places for snack stops. If you want a longer outing you can continue on the main trail that eventually ends at Elk Meadows (see No. 15).

Drive on Oregon 35 for 14 miles from its junction with US 26 or 25 miles south of Hood River to a large parking area off the west side of the highway where a sign states *East Fork Trail No. 650*. This turnout is 0.2 mile north of Sherwood Campground and 1.0 mile south of Polallie Campground.

The trail begins from the northwest edge of the turnout at a sign and winds through woods for a few hundred feet to a narrow footbridge over the East Fork of the Hood River. Hike parallel to the river and the highway for 0.4 mile, occasionally traveling at a gradual uphill grade, to the edge of the canyon formed by Cold Spring Creek. Here you can look across the highway to an impressive formation of columnar basalt.

Turn sharply west and traverse 150 yards to the junction of the trail from Polallie Campground. Keep left (straight), descend slightly and cross Cold Spring Creek on a footbridge. Climb moderately along the north bank of the creek, periodically passing through some brief swampy areas. The deep woods become somewhat more open as you hike up the canyon and the stream constantly is changing character.

Near the edge of a boulder field at 1.4 miles switchback right and after a short distance come to the junction of the trail to Elk Meadows. Turn left and traverse through woods to the upper portion of the boulder field. Cross the rocks below a high cliff band then reenter woods and continue along the slope for the final few hundred yards to the view of Tamanawas Falls. Originally it was called Gifford Falls after a photographer named B.A. Gifford. Although the topographic map shows Tamanawas spelled with a "u", an official decision has since been made to omit the "u" so the spelling will be consistent with other local names of Indian derivation, such as Clackamas.

36

Tamanawas Falls

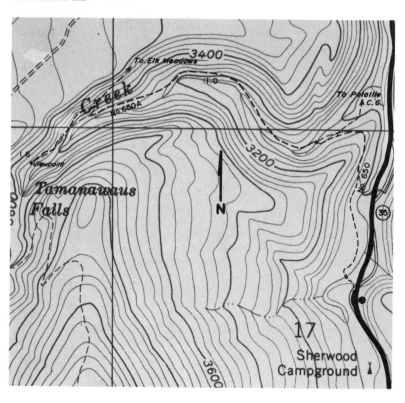

14 COOPER SPUR

One day trip
Distance: 3.5 miles one way
Elevation gain: 2,670 feet
High point: 8,514 feet
Allow 2½ to 3 hours one way
Usually open mid-July through early October
Topographic map:
U.S.G.S. Cathedral Ridge, Oreg.
7.5'   1962

Cooper Spur is the high, rocky ridge that separates Eliot and Newton Clark Glaciers on the northeast side of Mt. Hood. Eliot Glacier is the most extensive on the peak and also has the largest crevasses but even without the bird's-eye view of these yawning chasms the hike would be an exceptionally scenic trek. From near Cloud Cap Inn the route follows the Timberline Trail then winds up the barren, rocky spur toward the steep, fearsome north face of Mt. Hood. Start the hike with a full bottle of water as the sources along the route aren't dependable. This hike reaches the highest elevation in this guide.

Proceed on Oregon 35 for 15.5 miles from its junction with US 26 or 23.5 miles south of Hood River to a sign stating Tilly Jane Campground and Cooper Spur. Turn west and after 2.3 miles turn left, following the sign to Cloud Cap and Tilly Jane. Continue along S-12, that has a dirt surface after 1.4 miles, for 10 miles to the junction with the spur to Tilly Jane Camp-

ground. Keep right and continue up the final 0.8 mile to Cloud Cap Saddle Campground. If the few parking spaces off the road are taken, continue 0.2 mile to the large turnaround.

Walk about 200 feet through the campground to a three-way junction. For a description of the route of No. 600 to the right (west) see the Elk Cove to Cloud Cap subsection of No. 41. Keep straight (south) on No. 600 (don't take No. 600A down to Tilly Jane Campground), traverse through woods and then keep left on the main route at the junction of the side trail to Eliot Glacier. Continue up through woods of widely-spaced, thick-trunked alpine fir.

Come to a moraine at timberline and climb along the slopes of sand and boulders. Traverse the wall of a small rocky canyon where you might see, or at least hear, the whistle of marmots. Then curve left and climb through a swath of stunted white bark pine. Leave the trees and resume traversing a slope of rocks and scattered clumps of grass and other low growing plants. At 1.1 miles come to the junction of Trail No. 600A that also goes down to Tilly Jane Campground (see No. 12).

Turn right at the junction of No. 600A, leaving the Timberline Trail, and begin meandering up over rocky terrain. After a few hundred feet pass the remains of the Cooper Spur shelter off the trail to your right (north). The tread becomes more obvious as you gain elevation and the route travels parallel to and above the Timberline Trail for 1.0 mile beyond the junction.

At 2.2 miles begin the first of several long switchbacks. The trail engineers took the altitude into consideration and designed a steady, very moderate grade. During this methodical climb you can look north over the Upper and Lower Hood River Valleys to Mounts St. Helens, Rainier and Adams. The switchbacks become considerably shorter before you reach a good stopping place at 3.5 miles just before a dip in the crest. Elk Meadows (No's 15, 16, 17 and the Cloud Cap to Elk Meadows subsection of No. 41) to the southeast and Cloud Cap Inn on Ghost Ridge near the beginning of the hike are just two of the many landmarks you can identify from this lofty perch. You can continue along the crest for another 0.2 mile, passing Tie-In Rock where climbers traditionally put on their crampons and rope up, before reaching terrain that is unsuitable for hiking. Stay off any snow slopes as the surface probably will be hard and very slick.

Eliot Glacier from Cooper Spur

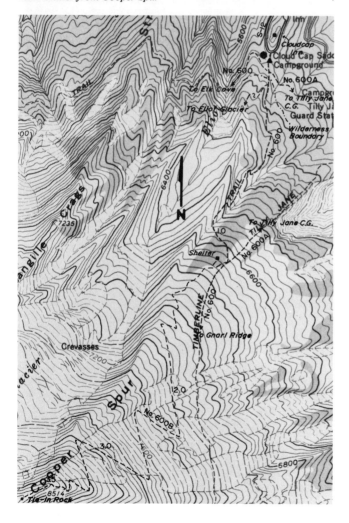

15 COLD SPRING CREEK TRAIL

One day trip or backpack
Distance: 7 miles one way
Elevation gain: 2,050 feet
High point: 5,050 feet
Allow 3½ hours one way
Usually open late June through October
Topographic maps:
  U.S.G.S. Badger Lake, Oreg.
  7.5'   1962
  U.S.G.S. Dog River, Oreg.
  7.5'   1962

The expansive Elk Meadows is the terminus of the Cold Spring Creek Trail and this huge grassy clearing below the east face of Mt. Hood is an enchanting place for an extended rest after the long, but gradual, climb. From the meadows you can hike 1.2 miles to the Timberline Trail and head north or south along this route that circles Mt. Hood. (See the Cloud Cap to Elk Meadows and Elk Meadows to Timberline Lodge subsections of No. 41.)

Cold Spring Creek Trail follows the western base of Bluegrass Ridge (No. 16) and you could return along its crest, rejoining the main trail at 2.7 miles. This loop would add about 0.8 mile and 600 feet of elevation gain. You also could return along the 2.9 miles long Elk Meadows Trail (No. 17) but this would necessitate a car shuttle.

Drive on Oregon 35 for 14 miles from its junction with US 25 or 25 miles south of Hood River to a large parking area off the west side of the highway where a sign states East Fork Trail No. 650. This turnout is 0.2 mile north of Sherwood Campground and 1.0 mile south of Polallie Campground.

The trail begins from the northwest edge of the turnout at a sign and winds through woods for a few hundred feet to a narrow footbridge across the East Fork of the Hood River. Hike parallel to the river and the highway for 0.4 mile, traveling gradually uphill, to the edge of the canyon formed by Cold Spring Creek.

Turn sharply west and traverse 150 yards to the junction of a trail from Polallie Campground. Keep left (straight), descend slightly and cross Cold Spring Creek on a footbridge. Climb moderately along the north bank of the creek, occasionally passing through some brief swampy areas. Near the edge of a boulder field at 1.4 miles switchback right and after a short distance come to the junction of the 0.2 mile spur to the viewpoint near the base of Tamanawas Falls (No. 13).

Turn right; after a few yards pass a pipe on your left and come to the crest of a ridge at the junction of a second trail to Polallie Campground. Turn left and walk along the broad, wooded crest then climb slightly to the unmarked junction of a trail to a jeep road that connects with the Cloud Cap Road, S-12. Keep left and resume climbing, passing through a semi-open area where you can see the intermontaine valley that separates Oregon 35 from the main slopes of Mt. Hood.

Drop slightly and come to the signed junction of Trail No. 644. Originally, this route was to have ended at Lamberson Butte (see No. 17) but construction was halted after 3.0 miles. Keep left and pass a sign indicating you're on Trail No. 645. Hike downhill and come to the junction of the Bluegrass Ridge Trail. If you make the possible loop, you'll be returning along this route.

Keep right and cross a stream on a small bridge then climb at an easy grade. At 3.4 miles come near the North Fork of Cold Spring Creek and cross it on a foot log. Continue climbing moderately through the forest with a few level stretches. Near 6.0 miles the grade becomes increasingly more gradual and eventually levels off. Come to the Perimeter Trail around Elk Meadows, keep right, cross a stream and reach the wooden shelter at the northern edge of the grass.

Hikers crossing Cold Spring Creek

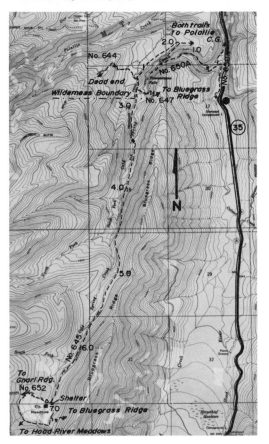

16 BLUEGRASS RIDGE

One day trip or backpack
Distance: 7.8 miles one way
Elevation gain: 2,780 feet; loss 500 feet
High point: 5,700 feet
Allow 3½ to 4 hours one way
Usually open July through October
Topographic maps:
  U.S.G.S. Badger Lake, Oreg.
  7.5'   1962
  U.S.G.S. Dog River, Oreg.
  7.5'   1962

This trail traverses almost the entire length of 4.5 mile long Bluegrass Ridge then winds down to Elk Meadows. You probably will want to spend considerable time at or near the shelter there lounging on the grass, enjoying the view of Newton Clark Glacier on the east face of Mt. Hood and investigating the meadow, the largest on the slopes of the peak. You can see some new scenery and save 0.7 mile of hiking and 500 feet of elevation gain by returning along the Cold Spring Creek Trail (No. 15). Also, by establishing a car shuttle, you could return along the 2.9 mile Elk Meadows Trail (No. 17).

Proceed on Oregon 35 for 14 miles from its junction with US 26 or 25 miles south of Hood River to a large parking area off the west side of the highway where a sign states *East Fork Trail*

No. 650. This turnout is 0.2 mile north of Sherwood Campground and 0.1 mile south of Polallie Campground.

The trail begins from the northwest edge of the turnout at a sign and winds through woods for a few hundred feet to a narrow footbridge across the East Fork of the Hood River. Hike parallel to the river and the highway for 0.4 mile at a gradual uphill grade to the edge of the canyon formed by Cold Spring Creek. Turn sharply west and traverse 150 yards to the junction of a trail from Polallie Campground. Keep left (straight), descend slightly and cross Cold Spring Creek on a footbridge. Climb at an erratic, but always moderate, grade beside the creek. Near the edge of a boulder field at 1.4 miles switchback right and after a short distance come to the junction of the 0.2 mile spur to Tamanawas Falls (No. 13).

Turn right, traverse uphill, curve left and come to the crest of a ridge at the junction of a second trail to Polallie Campground. Turn left and walk along the broad, wooded crest then climb slightly to an unmarked junction of a connector to Road S-12. Keep left, resume climbing then drop briefly and come to the signed junction of Trail No. 644 that ends after 3.0 miles. Keep left again and hike downhill to the junction of the Bluegrass Ridge Trail. The Cold Spring Creek Trail continues south to Elk Meadows and you'll be returning along it if you make the loop.

Turn left, drop a little then climb over a low hump. Cross a small stream just before coming to a bridge over the North Fork of Cold Spring Creek. Climb steeply then more moderately along the northwest end of Bluegrass Ridge to the crest and begin the 4.0 mile stretch along the mostly wooded ridge top. The moderate uphill grade occasionally is interrupted by brief stretches of downhill. Near 5.9 miles the route leaves the crest and traverses the east side of the slope for 1.1 miles.

Where you rejoin the ridge top at 7.0 miles you can turn right and walk back along the summit to a rocky viewpoint. One-tenth mile south of where you meet the crest come to the junction of the trail to Elk Mountain (see No. 17), keep right on 647B and begin winding steeply downhill for 0.3 mile. Where you come to the first open area keep along its left (south) edge then at a second, larger clearing follow the route marked by a few stakes. Intersect the Elk Meadows Perimeter Trail, turn right, walk to the junction of the Cold Spring Creek Trail No. 645, keep left and come to the shelter at the northeast corner of the meadow.

Hikers on Bluegrass Ridge

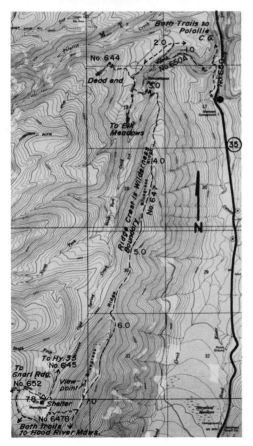

17 ELK MEADOWS and LAMBERSON BUTTE

One day trip or backpack
Distance: 5.3 miles one way
Elevation gain: 2,370 feet; loss 250 feet
High point: 6,633 feet
Allow 3 to 3½ hours one way
Usually open mid-July through mid-October
Topographic maps:
   U.S.G.S. Badger Lake, Oreg.
   7.5'   1962
   U.S.G.S. Mt. Hood South, Oreg.
   7.5'   1962

Scenic Elk Meadows is a good destination for those who don't want to complete the trip along Gnarl ridge to the impressive view of Newton Clark Glacier from Lamberson Butte. During 1978 Forest Service crews finished the last link of a trail that circles Elk Meadows and they also completed a connector, No. 652, to the Timberline Trail that by-passes the meadow. You also could make a side loop to Elk Mountain that would add 1.8 miles and 350 feet of uphill. An extremely attractive loop can be made west along the Timberline Trail No. 600 (see the Elk Meadows to Timberline Lodge subsection of No. 41) to the junction of Trail No. 646 and down it to the Elk Meadows Trail. This spectacular circuit would add only 1.0 mile and involve no extra climbing.

Drive on Oregon 35 for 7.2 miles east of its junction with US 26 or 32 miles south of Hood River to a sign pointing north to Hood River Meadows Campground. (Note: A new parking area for the ski area is being built just east of Hood River Meadows so this sign may be changed.) Turn north, after several yards turn left and proceed 0.3 mile to turnouts on either side of the road.

From the large sign at the northwest end of the parking area walk gradually uphill through woods for 0.3 mile to the junction of the trail to Umbrella Falls (No. 19). Keep right (straight) and a short distance farther pass the Wilderness register then come to the Wilderness boundary at Clark Creek. Veer right and descend to a footbridge. Head upstream several yards after the crossing then switchback right and travel on the level past a patch of huckleberry bushes.

At 1.0 mile come to the junction of the Newton Creek Trail No. 646, keep straight and after several hundred feet come to Newton Creek. Walk upstream 60 yards and cross the flow on a bridge. Climb in eight switchbacks then walk on the level for a few hundred feet to a four-way junction. The trail to the left (north) is the new alignment of the Gnarl Ridge Trail No. 652. It climbs through woods, passes some glimpses of Mt. Hood then continues up along more open slopes to the junction of the trail, No. 652A, from Elk Meadows.

If you intend to make the loop past Elk Mountain, turn right at the four-way junction onto the Bluegrass Ridge Trail No. 647 (No. 16). Climb 0.7 mile to a small clearing of beargrass then descend a short distance to the signed junction of the 0.1 mile spur to the site of the former lookout. Return the 0.1 mile to the junction, turn north and descend slightly before traversing uphill along the east side of a sparsely wooded slope. Follow the faint path over the crest and after several yards come to the junction of Trail No. 647B. Turn left and descend 0.3 mile to the Elk Meadows Perimeter Trail.

To go directly to Elk Meadows from the four-way junction at 2.1 miles, keep straight and descend gradually 0.2 mile to the Perimeter Trail. Turn right, after 0.6 mile pass Trail No. 647B, 0.2 mile farther keep left at the junction of the Cold Spring Creek Trail (No. 15) and come to the wooden shelter.

To reach Lamberson Butte from the shelter head northwest along Trail No. 652A. Enter woods, keep right where the Perimeter Trail heads south and climb 0.5 mile to the Gnarl Ridge Trail from the four-way junction. Continue up another 0.3 mile to the Timberline Trail, turn right and travel up through woods and periodic grassy areas. Just before 4.0 miles begin traversing the rocky, less vegetated northern slope of the ridge. Pass the remains of a stone shelter on your left and come to an excellent viewpoint at a crest vegetated with bush-like, gnarled white bark pine. To reach Lamberson Butte climb to the southeast for several hundred yards.

Mt. Hood from Hood River Meadows

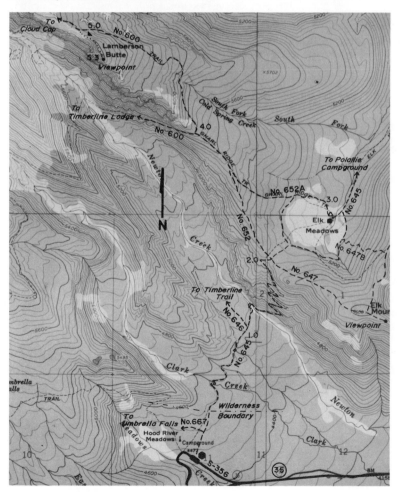

18 LOOKOUT MOUNTAIN

One day trip
Distance: 5.2 miles one way
Elevation gain: 2,975 feet
High point: 6,525 feet
Allow 2½ hours one way
Usually open late June through October
Topographic map:
  U.S.G.S. Badger Lake, Oreg.
  7.5'   1962

Although less than 10 miles east of Mt. Hood, the sections of grassy open slopes traversed along the middle third of the scenically delightful climb to Lookout Mountain are atypical of what usually is encountered in the northern Oregon Cascades. But even more noteworthy is the stupendous view from the summit. You'll see as far as Mounts St. Helens, Rainier and Adams in Washington, a section of the Columbia River east of The Dalles, over wheat fields to the Blue Mountains, to Lava Butte south of Bend, Broken Top, the Three Sisters, Mounts Washington and Jefferson and across the Cascade foothills to the Coast Range. Within this rim of the farthest landmarks you can study the Upper Hood River and Tygh Valleys, look down onto High Prairie and Badger Lake, directly to the north, identify high points in the Columbia Gorge, barely discern the two buildings at Cloud Cap and spot features to the west such as Bonney (No. 49) and Frog Lake (No. 51) Buttes.

You can shorten the hike to 2.6 miles with 1,300 feet of uphill by beginning from Road S-21 at Gumjuwac Saddle.

Proceed on Oregon 35 for 10 miles east from its junction with US 26 or 29 miles south of Hood River to a large sign on the east side of the highway stating *Gumjuwac Trail No. 480* and turn into a parking area. This is just south of the entrance to Robin Hood Campground across the highway. If you plan to begin the hike from Gumjuwac Saddle, drive on Oregon 35 6.2 miles east of its junction with US 26 to the Bennett Pass Road, S-21, across from the spur to Mt. Hood Meadows Ski Area. Follow S-21 4.2 miles to a junction and turn left. Continue along the rough, unpaved surface 5.0 miles, keeping left on S-21 where a road heads downhill, to the large wooden sign identifying Gumjuwac Saddle.

From the parking area off Oregon 35 cross the listing bridge, veer left and head several yards to the northeast corner of the clearing where the trail begins. Climb through woods in eight switchbacks. At 1.6 miles curve around to the north facing slope, switchback, and come to a rocky crest. Return to the north side and switchback again to the rocky ridge. Resume traveling along the north slope, pass above Jack Spring, an excellent source of cold water, and 200 yards farther come to Road S-21 at Gumjuwac Saddle.

Cross the road, turn left and head north along the Divide Trail No. 458. The other two routes descend to Badger Lake (No. 20). Walk on the level, occasionally near S-21, come to the first open area and begin climbing along the grassy slope that is bright with wildflowers early in the summer. The peak to the east with the lookout tower is Flag Point.

Enter woods, pass a spring that is not a dependable source of water and continue traversing. Switchback and resume hiking along a more open slope. Near 3.9 miles curve sharply right and travel along the wooded northwest slope. Switchback at the edge of a small scree field, traverse and curve back to the more open south side. Go into the head of a canyon and make four short switchbacks to a good viewpoint on the crest of the ridge. Curve right and walk along or near the crest for 0.2 mile to an old road, keep right and follow it the final 150 yards up to the summit.

Trail No. 458 resumes from the right side of the road just before you reach the summit and it can be taken back to Gumjuwac Saddle if you want to add 9.5 miles and 1,540 feet of climbing. Senecal Spring, a good source of water, is accessible along a path from Trail No. 458, but you'd have to lose 250 feet of elevation to reach it.

46

Old guard station at High Prairie

Looking east from Lookout Mountain

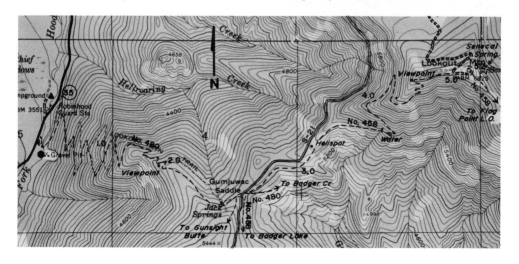

19 UMBRELLA FALLS LOOP

One day trip
Distance: 4.2 miles round trip
Elevation gain: 770 feet
High point: 5,250 feet
Allow 2½ hours round trip
Usually open June through October
Topographic map:
  U.S.G.S. Mt. Hood South, Oreg.
  7.5'   1962

In 1978, trail crews reopened part of a very old route and built sections of new tread so a scenic loop is now possible between Hood River Meadows and lovely Umbrella Falls on the southeast side of Mt. Hood.

Drive on Oregon 35 for 7.2 miles east of its junction with US 26 or 32 miles south of Hood River to a sign pointing north to Hood River Meadows Campground. (Note: A new parking area for the ski area is being built just east of Hood River Meadows so this sign may be changed.) Turn north, after several yards turn left and proceed 0.3 mile to turnouts on either side of the road.

From the large sign at the northwest end of the parking area walk gradually uphill through woods for 0.2 mile to the junction of Umbrella Falls Trail. Trail No. 645 continues to Elk Meadows (No. 17). (Note: Because the route of the eastern 0.3 mile of the Umbrella Falls Trail goes through land that eventually will be the parking lot serving the new chair lift at Mt. Hood Meadows Ski Area, this section is scheduled to be realigned in 1979 about 0.1 mile to the north. The route described below will be as it was in the fall of 1978 so what you may see between 0.2 and 0.9 mile and what is discussed in the text may not agree. However, the new route will be straightforward and easy to find. Just stay on Trail No. 645 until the signed junction, turn left onto the Umbrella Falls Trail and travel to the west.)

Turn left, walk on the level then travel slightly downhill to the junction of a trail back to the campground. Keep right and begin winding up. The realigned portion of the trail will meet the old route at the second turn at 0.9 miles. Traverse to the east and make two short switchbacks along an open slope. As you travel up the clearing you can look down on Hood River Meadows and see Bonney Butte (No. 49), the long, flat-topped ridge to the south.

Climb through woods and eventually pass under the chair lift. Traverse through a strip of woods and cross a wide run. Rise more noticeably, travel on the level briefly then begin descending gradually, occasionally passing through clearings thick with false hellebore. Cross a small stream and 0.2 mile farther come to another creek and the junction of the trail you'll be following if you make the loop.

To complete the hike to Umbrella Falls keep right and walk through deeper woods with slight ups and downs. Cross a small creek and a few hundred feet farther come to the bridge over the East Fork of the Hood River at the base of Umbrella Falls. The paved trail at the west end of the span climbs in three short switchbacks to the parking lot for the Mt. Hood Meadows Ski Area and the path to the left traverses for 0.1 mile to the spur road to the parking area.

To make the loop return to the junction at 2.0 miles and take the fork to the south. Descend gradually in woods, passing near a small meadow and crossing two small but very deeply channeled streams. Continue downhill and 1.0 mile from the junction cross a creek and traverse up to near a low ridge crest. Resume descending and travel above the narrow gorge formed by the East Fork of the Hood River.

Just beyond where you see a bridge on the old section of Oregon 35 have a glimpse of Sahalie Falls. Continue dropping and near 3.8 miles curve left onto an old road bed. Except for one brief uphill stretch follow it down to the old highway. Cross the pavement to the resumption of the trail and walk on the level through woods for 0.1 mile to the southwest edge of the parking area where you began.

Umbrella Falls

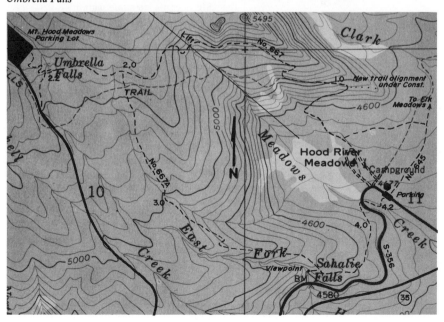

20 BADGER LAKE

One day trip or backpack
Distance: 6.5 miles one way
Elevation gain: 2,195 feet; loss 560 feet
High point: 5,220 feet
Allow 4 hours one way
Usually open July through October
Topographic map:
U.S.G.S. Badger Lake, Oreg.
7.5'   1962

In 1977 a long abandoned trail from Gumjuwac Saddle down to Badger Lake was reopened so now the hike to this lake can be done as a loop. You can shorten the trip by 2.2 miles and have 1,700 fewer feet of climbing by beginning from Road S-21 at the saddle.

Proceed on Oregon 35 for 10 miles east from its junction with US 26 or 29 miles south of Hood River to a large sign on the east side of the highway stating *Gumjuwac Trail No. 480* and turn into a parking area. This is just south of the entrance to Robin Hood Campground across the highway. If you plan to begin the hike from Gumjuwac Saddle, drive on Oregon 35 6.2 miles east of its junction with US 26 to the Bennett Pass Road, S-21, across from the spur to Mt. Hood Meadows Ski Area. Follow S-21 4.2 miles to a junction and turn left. Continue along the rough, unpaved surface 5.0 miles, keeping left on S-21 where a road heads

downhill, to the large wooden sign identifying Gumjuwac Saddle.

From the parking area off Oregon 35 cross the listing bridge, veer left and head several yards to the northeast corner of the clearing where the trail begins. Climb through woods in eight switchbacks. At 1.6 miles curve around to the north facing slope, switchback and come to a rocky crest. Return to the north side and switchback again to the rocky ridge. Resume traveling along the north slope, pass above Jack Spring and 200 yards farther come to Road S-21 at Gumjuwac Saddle.

Cross S-21 to the continuation of Trail No. 480. Trail No. 458 just to the right (south) is the recently reopened route to Badger Lake and is shorter by 2.0 miles. The trail several yards north along S-21 climbs to Lookout Mountain (No. 18).

If you plan to follow No. 480, walk downhill in woods for a couple hundred feet then descend steeply through a meadow. The first 0.2 mile of No. 480 is scheduled to be rebuilt in 1979 and this steep stretch will be avoided. Be watching for a few aspen, a beautiful deciduous tree lamentably scarce in the northern Oregon Cascades. Continue down in woods, hop a small stream and at 3.5 miles cross a larger flow. At a signed but abandoned trail keep right and 0.1 mile farther come to Trail No. 479 that also heads to the Flag Point Road.

Turn right and cross Gumjuwac Creek. Soon begin climbing near Badger Creek and cross a few side streams. Resume walking on the level and 2.0 miles from the junction at Gumjuwac Creek come to a sign marking the short connector to Road S-340. Keep straight (right) and begin traversing up along a more open slope. Reenter deeper woods, at the junction of the 50 yard spur to the dam keep right again and continue up for 0.1 mile to the possibly unsigned junction of Trail No. 458 that climbs back to Gumjuwac Saddle. The trail that continues straight ends at Road S-339 after 1.2 miles.

If you want to have lunch at the lake turn left at the junction of Trail No. 458 at 6.6 miles and descend several hundred feet to the shore.

To make the loop, turn right (north) onto Trail No. 458 and climb, occasionally at a moderately steep angle. Cross two small side streams and continue uphill, but at a gentler grade. Traverse a more open area where you can see down over Badger Lake and east toward Condon. Go over a crest and as you descend have a view northeast to Lookout Mountain. Climb gradually then drop a last time, traveling just below S-21, to Gumjuwac Saddle.

Badger Lake

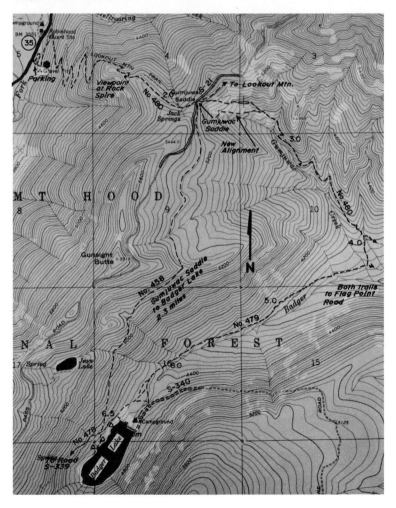

21 WILDCAT MOUNTAIN

One day trip
Distance: 5 miles one way
Elevation gain: 1,700 feet; loss 100 feet
High point: 4,481 feet
Allow 2½ to 3 hours one way
Usually open June through November
Topographic map:
  U.S.G.S. Cherryville, Oreg.
  15'   1955

Wildcat Mountain is a long north-south oriented ridge in the westernmost foothills of the Cascades and the view along the summit crest affords some uncommon perspectives. You'll be able to see the tallest buildings of Portland, the Trojan nuclear facility on the Columbia River, the Goat Rocks east of Mt. Adams and southwest to Marys Peak in the Coast Range as well as the more conventional landmarks such as Mounts St. Helens, Adams, Hood and Jefferson, Olallie Butte (No. 60), Bull of the Woods (No. 56) and high points in the Columbia Gorge such as Larch Mountain and Tanner Butte.

If you wanted to establish a car shuttle, you could head southeast from the viewpoint at 5.0 miles for 1.0 mile to the junction of Trail No. 783, turn left and travel another 1.5 miles to the junction of the Bonanza Trail (No. 22). You could reach the summit of Wildcat Mountain

from the west along a shorter route but it is considerably less scenic, the beginning is time consuming to reach and, unfortunately, the trail may be open to motorized travel. Carry water as no sources are available along the hike.

Drive on US 26 for 10.5 miles east of Sandy or 7.5 miles west of Zigzag to narrow, unpaved E. Wildcat Creek Road, 0.8 miles east of the 35 mile post heading south from the highway. Turn onto it and proceed 3.0 miles to a fork. Keep right and after 50 feet come to a sign on your left identifying the start of the Wildcat Trail. The best parking usually is back down the road just below the fork.

Climb somewhat steeply through a narrow corridor of small trees to the ridge crest. Follow a mostly gradual grade through a coniferous forest that varies surprisingly in character, from the deep green of the dense woods to the chartreuse hue in sections of thin, widely spaced and moss covered trees. Rhododendron bushes, with their big pink blooms best around late June, frequent the latter areas.

Rise more noticeably and at 2.0 miles come to a good viewpoint of Mt. Hood. Note where the trail enters a clearing so you'll be able to locate it on your return. Continue across the open area in the same direction you were heading and resume climbing in woods. Come to signs identifying the route of long abandoned Alder Creek Way No. 2 and continue uphill along the main trail.

Traverse under a rocky ridge, climb steeply then come to a field of thick beargrass. Individual beargrass clumps do not bloom every year and the best displays in a given area tend to be in biennial cycles. (1978 was a stupendous year. Bears do indeed eat the plants, particularly the base and another name, squawgrass, is also apt as Indian women used the blades for weaving baskets and clothing.) Come to a fork where a path loops left past a viewpoint and rejoins the main trail. If you want to visit the overlook, make the side trip now as the south fork is obscure when you're heading north. Climb gradually along the main trail through sparse woods to an open crest where you'll have those good views to the west. Walk on the level, drop slightly then traverse to the junction with Trail No. 781 that descends west to an access road.

Turn left and climb toward the summit of Wildcat Mountain. Where the route levels off and contours below the top look right for a possibly unsigned spur heading up to the site of the lookout tower that was removed in the early 1950's.

Relaxing in the meadows

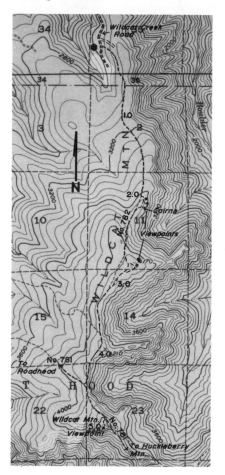

22 BONANZA TRAIL

One day trip
Distance: 4.8 miles one way
Elevation gain: 3,000 feet
High point: 4,350 feet
Allow 3 hours one way
Usually open mid-June through October
Topographic maps:
  U.S.G.S. Cherryville, Oreg.
  15   1955
  U.S.G.S. Rhododendron, Oreg.
  7.5'   1962

Three trails in this guide pass old mines; the Pioneer Bridle Trail (No. 37), the one to Pansy Basin and Bull of the Woods (No. 56) and the Bonanza Trail. The diggings along the first two, though certainly interesting and uncommon, are not especially impressive. But, the Bonanza Mine has a large, proper tunnel complete with old tracks. Another shaft is just a short distance off the trail from the first switchback.

The hike ends on Huckleberry Mountain, a long, wooded ridge in the Salmon River drainage south of Rhododendron. From the crest you'll have views over the surrounding terrain and west to the Columbia River and the plumes of smoke that identify the paper mill at Camas, Washington. In 1979 trail crews are scheduled to begin construction on a new section of the Plaza Trail No. 783 that goes north along the crest of Huckleberry Mountain. When completed it will connect somewhere along the first mile of the Bonanza Trail so a fine loop will be possible. A trail sign at the junction will indicate that the work has been completed.

Proceed on US 26 17 miles east of Sandy or 1.0 mile west of Zigzag to the road to Welches at the Hoodland shopping complex. Turn south and travel past the golf course, in its pre-manicured days called Welches Bottom then Billy's Calf Pasture, to a fork 1.2 miles from the highway. Keep left at the fork and 0.6 mile farther keep straight where a sign says *One Lane Bridge* and cross. Several yards beyond the span stay straight (right) then turn left several yards farther and follow a narrow, rough and chuck-holed, but level, road 0.3 mile to a sign on your right marking the beginning of the Bonanza Trail.

Walk along an old roadbed and after a short distance cross a dilapidated bridge. Continue following the level road for 0.8 mile then just beyond where you come near Cheeney Creek look for an overgrown road heading up to the right. Veer onto it and pass a sign identifying the route of the Bonanza Trail. After several yards keep straight (left) where a road joins then farther on veer right where a road merges from the downslope side. This first part of the trip is through alder woods, an airy, delicate contrast to the more sedate coniferous forest along most of the climb.

Drop slightly, now traveling on a trail through a mixture of cedar, fir, maple and ferns, and cross a stream. Several yards beyond the ford keep right where a spur heads down to a campsite. Traverse above Cheeney Creek at an erratic, but always moderate, grade of up, down and level stretches. The grade eventually steepens and at 1.9 miles the trail switchbacks. After a long traverse switchback again and farther on curve around the face of a slope. Rhododendron bushes and beargrass become increasingly dense beyond here.

Enter a side canyon and at its head cross a stream, the last source of water, and pass the entrance of the mine tunnel. Hike on the level out of the side canyon, round the face of a slope and resume climbing. Make eight switchbacks along or near a crest then again traverse and round the face of another slope. At one open area you can see the summit of Huckleberry Mountain ahead across the canyon.

Come to a long saddle and cross it, losing a few feet of elevation, then resume climbing and come to the junction of the Plaza Trail. The route that heads south (straight) goes to Wildcat Mountain (No. 21). To reach the summit of Huckleberry Mountain turn right and climb about 0.2 mile to the first viewpoint. An even better one is several hundred feet farther along the trail. Continue along the trail to a more open, rocky area on the crest where you can see down into the Salmon River Valley and the route of the Bonanza Trail.

Summit of Huckleberry Mountain

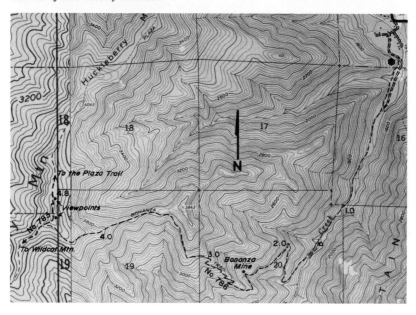

23 HUNCHBACK MOUNTAIN

One day trip
Distance: 4.5 miles one way
Elevation gain: 2,850 feet; loss 210 feet
High point: 4,033 feet
Allow 3 to 4 hours one way
Usually open June through November
Topographic map:
  U.S.G.S. Rhododendron, Oreg.
  7.5'   1962

Hunchback Mountain is the long, wooded ridge that begins at the community of Zigzag and extends 10 miles southeast to Devils Peak (No. 36). Pyramid Viewpoint at 4.5 miles is a good destination or you could establish a car shuttle and traverse the entire length of the ridge. This one way trip would add 5.0 miles and 1,580 feet of uphill hiking than if you retraced your route. The first 2.0 miles climb at a frequently steep grade and a few stretches farther on also rise at a severe angle so your leg muscles will get a workout on this hike. Carry water.

Drive on US 26 18 miles east of Sandy or 2.0 miles west of Rhododendron to the Zigzag Ranger Station off the south side of the highway and leave your car at the east end of the large parking area.

Walk east from the parking area along an old roadbed for a few hundred feet to an unmarked trail on your right. Follow it 25 yards to another old roadbed. Cross it and come to the beginning of the Hunchback Trail. Climb about 100 yards and switchback just below a cistern. Continue up through woods in three more switchbacks to a bench at 0.3 mile. Resume climbing in 13 switchbacks then curve sharply left and hike up along the crest. Traverse along the west side of the ridge and have a view of Huckleberry Mountain (see No. 22) to the southwest. Drop slightly then resume climbing at a sometimes steep grade and enter the beargrass and rhododendron zone. At 2.2 miles come to a viewpoint at a rocky, open and narrow section of the crest. These several yards are very exposed, so be careful.

Descend briefly, reenter woods and resume climbing. At the top of a steep pitch come to a sign stating *Viewpoint Rockpile.* If you want to see Washbowl Rock there, turn right and climb steeply about 200 feet to a sign identifying the route. Turn right and follow the short path to the edge of a boulderfield then continue up to a cluster of rocks on the crest.

The main trail continues traversing the east slope. You can see Mt. Hood and down onto the buildings at the west end of Rhododendron. Again climb very steeply, cross a patch of scree then hike gradually up along the crest that is now considerably broader. This respite eventually ends and the trail again rises steeply. Traverse along the north side to a sign pointing to Viewpoint-Helispot 260. This overlook offers the most extensive views of the hike and if you want to visit it continue along the main trail about 70 feet then turn right and climb to the crest. Turn left at the ridge top and go to the helispot site. In addition to Mt. Hood you can see Cast (No. 29) and East Zigzag (No. 31) Mountains, the wooded expanse of the Salmon-Huckleberry area to the west, Salmon Butte (No. 25), east up Still Creek Valley and down onto Flag Mountain (No. 35) and US 26.

The main trail alternates between climbing and descending and follows the crest or traverses the east slope. Come to a more open area on the crest at the base of some pinnacles. Make the last series of steep climbs along the ridge top then begin descending. Where you come to the first switchback continue straight, as indicated by the sign pointing to Viewpoint—Great Pyramid, for 50 yards to the overlook where you can see the resort at Welches, west down the Sandy River valley and Larch Mountain in the Columbia Gorge. The main trail continues downhill for 0.4 mile then climbs 5.1 miles to the junction with the short spur to Devils Peak.

Rock spires along the ridge

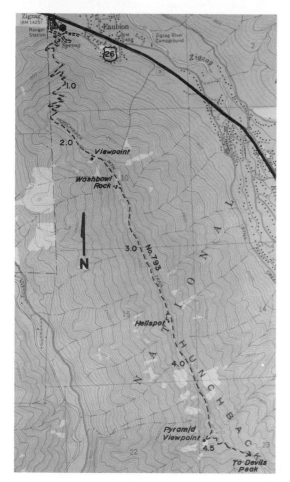

24 OLD SALMON RIVER TRAIL

One-half day trip
Distance: 2.6 miles one way
Elevation gain: 100 feet
High point: 1,640 feet
Allow 1½ hours one way
Usually open late February through December
Topographic map:
U.S.G.S. Rhododendron, Oreg.
7.5'   1962

A trail once paralleled the Salmon River all the way from the community of Welches to Government Camp but the construction of Road S-38 disrupted some of the first 4.0 miles of the original route. However, a portion of the northernmost section of the Old Salmon River Trail still provides more than 2.5 miles of easy, scenic hiking. Although S-38 is glimpsed several times and the route actually follows the road twice for a few hundred yards, the deep, lush woods and the constant proximity of the rushing Salmon River usually create the effect of being far from civilization. For the return portion of the hike you can retrace your steps, establish a car shuttle or hike back along the road.

On US 26, proceed 17.9 miles east of Sandy or 0.1 mile west of Zigzag to the Salmon River Road, S-38, at mile post 42 and turn south. Drive 2.6 miles, keeping left where a road goes downhill, and 500 feet beyond the sign marking the boundary of the Mt. Hood National Forest come to a sign on the right (west) side of the road identifying the beginning of the hike. If you plan to establish a car shuttle, continue 2.4 miles farther along S-38 to the turnouts before the bridge over the Salmon River.

Descend slightly then travel through moss encrusted woods. Cross a small stream and continue hiking through the rain forest. Although the evergreens aren't especially close together, hanging moss and the carpet of ferns create a dense, lush environment. Walk parallel to the Salmon River and come to a more open area where sorrel, larkspur and other wildflowers bloom during early spring.

At 0.5 mile cross a former bed of the Salmon River then curve away from the main flow and recross the old bed. Climb the steep bank and resume walking in a southerly direction. Cross a partially collapsed bridge near 0.8 mile and after traversing along the bank come to a junction a few hundred feet east of the river. The path to the right goes to a place in the river where the flow of the water is slowed by a deep hole.

Bear left to stay on the main route and near 1.0 mile travel on a faint, old roadbed. Keep right on a path and after a few hundred feet meet a more obvious, but also abandoned, old vehicle way and keep straight. Cross a wide, shallow stream and a short distance farther be watching for and follow a path that veers right and is marked by swaths of blue paint sprayed on tree trunks.

At 1.4 miles meet Road S-38 and walk along its shoulder for 0.1 mile for the length of a retaining wall. In many of the sunny areas along the roadbed coltsfoot thrive and the cluster of cream-colored blossoms at the end of the thick stalks are easy to identify. Immediately at the end of the wall drop along an unmarked path back to river level. Soon reenter a mossy forest and follow the winding trail near the stream. Where you come near the road stay right along the edge of the bank.

Come to the northwestern edge of Green Canyon Campground at 2.0 miles and keep right near the bank. A short distance beyond its south end climb several yards to S-38. Walk along the shoulder for 100 yards then descend along the obvious path that leaves the road at a shallow angle. Continue through woods 0.3 mile to the end of the hike at S-38. The Salmon River Trail (No. 26) resumes across the road.

Fisherman on Salmon River

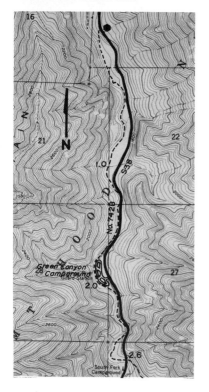

Salmon River

59

25 SALMON BUTTE

One day trip
Distance: 4.3 miles one way
Elevation gain: 2,800 feet
High point: 4,877 feet
Allow 2½ to 3½ hours one way
Usually open June through October
Topographic maps:
    U.S.G.S. High Rock, Oreg.
    15'   1956
    U.S.G.S. Rhododendron, Oreg.
    7.5'   1962

The climb to the rocky, treeless summit of Salmon Butte is one of the most scenic and enjoyable of the trips in the foothills southwest of Mt. Hood. The route generally travels through woods of varying, but always attractive, character until reaching the top where the view extends from Mounts St. Helens, Rainier and Adams along the northern horizon, over landmarks in the Columbia Gorge and past the southwest face of Mt. Hood to Mt. Jefferson on the southern skyline. During mid-July your progress through the clearcut at the beginning of the hike may be slowed by the abundance of succulent, tiny wild blackberries. Fill your bottle before leaving home as the water sources along the trail may not be dependable all season.

Drive on US 26 17.9 miles east of Sandy or 0.1 mile west of Zigzag to the Salmon River Road, S-38, at mile post 42 and turn south. Follow S-38, keeping left where a road goes downhill, for 5.0 miles to a bridge. Six-tenths mile farther come to another span and 1.1 miles beyond it come to a logging spur on your right where a sign identifies the beginning of the Salmon Butte Trail. Parking spaces are available along the shoulder of S-38.

Walk up the logging spur for about 100 yards and just before the end of the roadbed be looking to your left for the signed trailhead. Turn left here and follow the path up through the clearcut. The formal trail begins from the edge of the woods at the southern, upper end of the logged area and climbs moderately through the deep forest.

At 1.0 mile cross the face of a ridge and travel through less lush woods to the junction of an unmaintained trail to Mack Hall Creek. Keep left and 0.2 mile farther come to a viewpoint at a small, open rocky area. Reenter woods and continue traversing. At 1.7 miles hop a small side stream then cross the face of another ridge. Make two short switchbacks and come to a second stream. Continue traversing then make four switchbacks of varying lengths and at 3.2 miles abruptly cross to the east side of the summit ridge.

After a couple hundred feet come to an open area that affords a view of the southwest face of Mt. Hood. Reenter woods and begin climbing along a narrow portion of the crest. The ridge broadens and the trail passes a third possible source of water. Traverse through a brushy area, curve right and make one switchback along a timbered slope with no groundcover. Climb through a patch of rhododendron bushes, wind up for several yards and come to Road S-409.

Turn right and follow the road for 0.2 mile as it winds around the summit cone of Salmon Butte to its end just below the site of the former lookout cabin. In addition to the major peaks, you can identify lesser highpoints such as Silver Star Mountain in Washington, Larch and Chinidere (No. 2) Mountains, Palmer and Tanner Buttes and Mt. Defiance in the Columbia Gorge, Wildcat Mountain (No. 21) and Devils Peak (No. 36) nearby to the west and east and Signal and Olallie (No. 60) Buttes to the south.

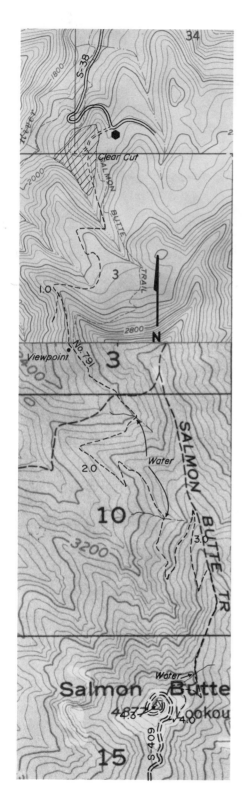

Mt. Hood from Salmon Butte

26 SALMON RIVER TRAIL

One day trip
Distance: 3.7 miles one way (to second View-
point)
Elevation gain: 950 feet; loss 400 feet (to sec-
ond Viewpoint)
High point: 2,490 feet
Allow 2 to 2½ hours one way
Usually open March through December
Topographic map:
   U.S.G.S. Rhododendron, Oreg.
   7.5'   1962

Woods along Salmon River

The Salmon River Trail is the continuation of the Old Salmon River Trail (No. 24) and parallels the robust stream for 14 miles before veering north and ending at a logging spur 7.0 miles from Government Camp. A use-path descends from the main trail at 3.5 miles to a steep, grassy slope that affords a good stopping place and a fine view of Final and Frustration Falls. During late spring the blossoms of columbine, larkspur, penstemon, Indian paintbrush and other bright wildflowers add color to the predominant greens of the mosses, ferns and trees and as the trail gains elevation the woods are sprinkled in early June with the delicate pink blooms of rhododendron bushes. Carry water later in the season as the several small streams along the route may not be dependable all year. Because of its relatively low elevation, the two Salmon River Trails can be done earlier and later in the year than most of the other hikes in this guide.

Proceed on US 26 17.9 miles east of Sandy or 0.1 mile west of Zigzag to the Salmon River Road, S-38, at mile post 42 and turn south. Drive 5.0 miles, keeping left where a road goes downhill, to turnouts on both sides of S-38 just before a bridge over the Salmon River. A sign on the east shoulder near the end of the span marks the trailhead.

Climb a short distance then hike with brief ups and downs through woods. The route vascillates between traveling beside and several hundred feet from the water's edge. At 1.7 miles pass Bighorn Campground then 0.5 mile farther come to Rolling Riffle Campground. Continue on the level for a short distance then begin climbing away from the river along a slope of Douglas fir and rhododendron and a few huckleberry bushes.

Near 3.2 miles come to the junction of the Viewpoint Trail that traverses a grassy slope with fine views and rejoin the main route in 0.2 miles. This is a scenic place to end the hike if you don't want to visit the viewpoint 0.5 mile farther.

Climb in and out of a side canyon and traverse across the face of a broad ridge. Where the trail levels off and begins to descend look right for an unmarked but well-defined path heading downslope. Turn right and drop through woods about 100 feet then where the slope becomes steep turn right. Descend steeply for a short distance, curve right and contour around the ridge crest. Hike down the grassy, open slope, bearing slightly left, until you can see Final Falls and Frustration Falls (so-named because it once was so hard to reach) cascading down the steep, rocky wall to the east. A good spot for a lunch stop is downslope on a grassy bench.

Salmon River Canyon

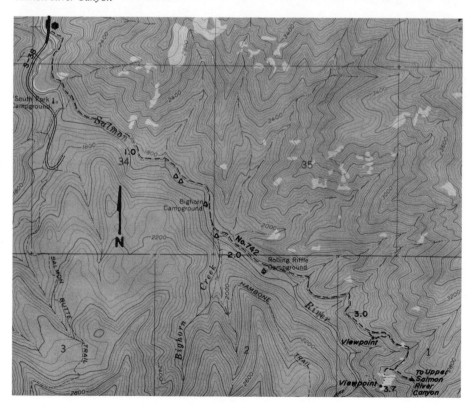

27 CASTLE CANYON

One-half day trip
Distance: 0.9 mile one way
Elevation gain: 850 feet
High point: 2,450 feet
Allow 45 minutes to 1 hour one way
Usually open March through November
Topographic map:
  U.S.G.S. Rhododendron, Oreg.
  7.5'   1962

Castle Canyon was named for the spire-shaped outcroppings of alluvial conglomerate protruding from the wooded southern slope of West Zigzag Mountain between the 1,800 and 2,800 foot levels. Some geologists think this area once was a lateral moraine of the Zigzag Glacier. Although the hike through this interesting region is less than 1.0 mile in length, the path climbs very steeply for most of its distance. Carry water as none is available along the trip.

On US 26, drive 18 miles east of Sandy or 2.0 miles west of Rhododendron to the community of Zigzag and turn north on the Lolo Pass Road. Proceed 0.4 mile to a road on your right identified as Road 19. Turn right, after 0.2 mile keep straight (right) at a fork and continue 1.4 miles to a sign on your left stating Castle Canyon Trail. Since Road 19 continues east a short distance to Rhododendron, you don't need to turn your car around after the hike. You can approach from the east by turning north onto Henry Creek Road and Little Brook Lane at the west end of Rhododendron. After a few yards turn left onto Henry Creek Road, go 0.3 mile to a fork, turn left onto Road 19 and drive 0.4 mile to the trailhead.

Climb gradually along a wooded slope that was selectively logged using draft horses to haul away the felled trees. After a few hundred yards cross a narrow old roadbed and continue up at a moderate grade. At the top end of the logged area begin climbing more noticeably in short switchbacks. Continue winding up at an increasingly steeper grade and reach a ridge crest.

At 0.5 mile come to the first of the exposed rocks. Continue up the narrow ridge crest then travel around the right side of an outcropping. Follow the narrow path that climbs steeply along the eastern base of the high, rock wall. Just below a little saddle a side path goes right for 100 feet to a small notch overlooking more formations.

From the saddle climb very steeply for a few hundred feet to a crest. You then can continue up the ridge for several hundred yards to a higher viewpoint. To reach the narrow, exposed rocky crest below to the south, descend the way you scrambled up for a couple hundred feet then turn right and traverse to the rocky spine. The site of the former lookout on West Zigzag Mountain (No. 28) can be seen above to the northeast and several populated areas along US 26 are visible below to the southwest.

The Castles

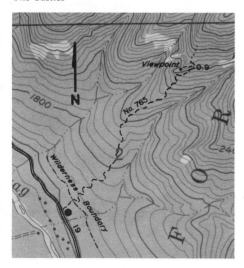

28 WEST ZIGZAG MOUNTAIN

One day trip
Distance: 5 miles one way
Elevation gain: 3,400 feet; loss 340 feet
High point: 4,525 feet
Allow 3 to 3½ hours one way
Usually open June through mid-November
Topographic map:
  U.S.G.S. Rhododendron, Oreg.
  7.5'   1962

West Zigzag Mountain looms 3,000 feet above the community of Rhododendron and the hike to its summit is a perfect choice when you want a moderately strenuous, easily accessible trip with good scenery. Carry water. A complex network of trails crisscrosses the area between West and East Zigzag Mountains and by establishing a car shuttle you can make one of five one-way trips. (Refer to No's. 29, 30, 31 and 34.) Or, you can shorten the return to 2.5 miles by following Trail No. 789 down to Road S-27 (see No. 34).

Proceed on US 26 18 miles east of Sandy or 2.0 miles west of Rhododendron to the community of Zigzag and turn north onto the Lolo Pass Road. Four-tenths mile from the highway look for a sign on your right stating Road 19 and turn onto it. After 0.2 mile keep straight (right) at a fork and continue 0.4 mile to a sign on your left that identifies the beginning of the Zigzag Mountain Trail. A turnout east of the sign provides a few parking spaces. You also can approach from the east by turning north onto Henry Creek Road and Little Brook Lane at the west end of Rhododendron. After a few yards turn left onto Henry Creek Road and 0.3 miles farther come to a fork. Turn left onto Road 19 and drive 1.4 miles to the trailhead.

Traverse uphill for a short distance then for the next 1.0 mile switchback at a steady, moderate grade. Come to a viewpoint where you can see down onto Rhododendron and across to Hunchback Mountain (No. 23) and Devils Peak (No. 36). Several yards farther

come to the crest and climb along or just below it in traverses and switchbacks for 1.5 miles. At 2.5 miles the trail crosses to the west side of the slope. Switchback and resume traveling on the wall of the huge basin. Switchback twice more and make a long traverse. At 2.9 miles go over the crest and have a view north to the vicinity of Lolo Pass.

Hike along the crest in a series of short ups and downs, climbing steeply for one brief stretch, then make three short switchbacks and resume traversing. Walk along a less densely vegetated portion of the crest and come to a good view of Mt. Hood. Drop slightly, travel on the crest then along the north side of the slope and begin a gradual descent. Come to a saddle at 4.1 miles where you can see your destination at the top of the high cliffs to the southwest.

Continue dropping gradually along the crest then curve left and enter deeper woods. Switchback right and come to a treeless viewpoint. Wind up the open slope in several short switchbacks then resume hiking along the north side of the slope. Traverse above a little basin then begin descending gradually. Drop steeply for about 150 feet, curve left and walk along the base of a sheer rock wall. Climb in short switchbacks then walk downhill for a few hundred feet. Where the trail curves sharply left turn right and drop for a few yards to reach the site of the former lookout. Castle Canyon (No. 27) is below to the west, the Salmon and Sandy River Valleys are beyond and the view extends south to Olallie Butte (No. 60) and Mt. Jefferson.

If you're planning to make any of the one way trips, continue along the main trail. Where you come near the crest leave the tread for a good view of Mounts Hood, St. Helens, Rainier and Adams. Several hundred yards from the lookout site come to the junction of Trail No. 789. Keep right if you want to make the shortest loop or stay left for the others.

Aerial view, West Zigzag Mountain

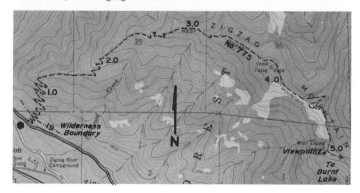

29 HORSESHOE RIDGE

One day trip
Distance: 3.3 miles one way
Elevation gain: 2,100 feet
High point: 4,877 feet
Allow 2½ to 3 hours one way
Usually open late June through October
Topographic map:
  U.S.G.S. Government Camp, Oreg.
  7.5'   1962

The Horseshoe Ridge Trail is one of several approaches to the maze of routes in the Zigzag Mountain area at the western end of the Mt. Hood Wilderness (see No's. 28, 30, 31 and 34). All the hikes in the region offer fine views that extend north to Mt. Rainier and south to Mt. Jefferson and the southwest face of Mt. Hood is only eight miles away. But the unique feature of the Zigzag Mountain area is the profusion of huckleberry bushes whose fruit ripens in late August or early September. If you do the trip then carry a container and allow extra time because those berries are irresistible.

Because of the network of routes, several loop trips are possible but the most efficient circuit is to combine the Horseshoe Ridge and Cast Creek (No. 30) Trails. If you have any knee problems, you'll probably want to do the Cast Creek Trail first as it has stretches of very steep grade. Since the two trailheads are only 1.5 miles apart you can do the loop without establishing a car shuttle. Carry water.

Drive on US 26 18 miles east of Sandy or 2.0 miles west of Rhododendron to the community of Zigzag and turn north on the Lolo Pass Road. Four miles from the highway turn right on the road to McNeil Campground and the Ramona Falls Trail. Go downhill 0.6 mile, turn right and cross a bridge. Four-tenths mile from the span turn right onto Road S-25D to Riley Campground and Horseshoe Trail. One-tenth mile farther keep left at the entrance to the campground and follow the unpaved road. After 0.5 mile pass the beginning of the Cast Creek Trail and 1.5 miles farther come to a sign identifying the Horseshoe Trail No. 774.

Climb 100 feet along the bank, curve left at the Wilderness register and continue up through woods at a moderate grade in 12 long switchbacks. Just beyond 1.0 mile pass a sign marking the Wilderness boundary and a little farther traverse beneath a rock pinnacle. Continue winding up in irregularly spaced switchbacks, alternating between the west and north slopes of Horseshoe Ridge. A few more rock clusters with attendant vine maple add scenic variety.

At 2.0 miles begin traveling at a gradual grade along the crest of the ridge and eventually have a view of Mt. Hood. Make two short switchbacks and continue on the crest through thinning trees to a viewpoint where you'll be able to see Mounts St. Helens, Rainier and Adams, Bald Mountain (No. 8) with a section of the Pacific Crest Trail (see the Ramona Falls to Cairn Basin subsection of No. 41) traversing across its south face and down onto Dumbbell Lake. You'll meet the first of the huckleberry bushes here.

Curve right and traverse along an open, rocky slope to the crest of the long east-west oriented ridge called Zigzag Mountain. The trail to the right reaches West Zigzag Mountain (No. 28) in 2.0 miles. From the junction you can see south to Olallie Butte (No. 60) and Mt. Jefferson and north to Larch Mountain and other landmarks in the Columbia Gorge.

Turn left and travel up the crest of grass and beargrass. Three-tenths mile from the junction come to the path on your left up to the viewpoint at 3.3 miles. The main trail continues traversing then follows the crest of a ridge as it curves to the southeast. If you follow it you'll be able to look down onto Cast Lake, ahead to East Zigzag Mountain (No. 31) and south to Barlow (No. 48) and Bonney (No. 49) Buttes. The trail traverses below the summit of Cast Mountain then descends for 0.6 mile to the junction of Trail No. 767 (see No. 34).

Trail sign at ridge top

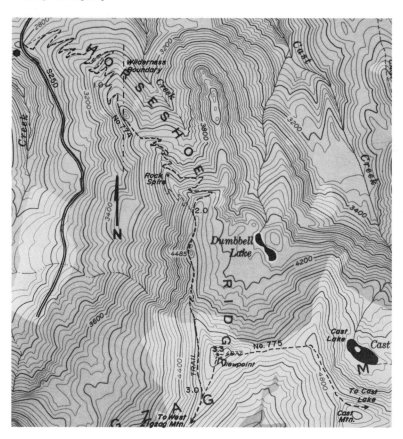

30 CAST CREEK TRAIL

One day trip or backpack
Distance: 4.5 miles one way
Elevation gain: 2,750 feet; loss 320 feet
High point: 4,600 feet
Allow 3 hours one way
Usually open late June through October
Topographic maps:
  U.S.G.S. Bull Run Lake, Oreg.
  7.5'   1962
  U.S.G.S. Government Camp, Oreg.
  7.5'   1962

Beavers have been busy around Cast Lake and you can study their handiwork at the dam they've built across the outlet. Another special feature of the hike is the number of huckleberry bushes you pass between 3.0 and 4.0 miles. The crop ripens around late August or early September, depending upon the weather conditions the preceding months. Since the berry fields extend east and south you can follow other trails through the area for an even bigger harvest (see No's. 29, 31 and 34).

This network of routes affords many loop trip possibilities. The most efficient pairing is to combine the Cast Creek and Horseshoe Ridge (No. 29) Trails. The entire circuit involves 9.0 miles with 3,500 feet of climbing. If you don't mind an extra 1.5 miles along a road, you don't even need to establish a car shuttle. Water is not available along the hike so carry an adequate supply.

Proceed on US 26 18 miles east of Sandy or 2.0 miles west of Rhododendron to the community of Zigzag and turn north onto the Lolo Pass Road. Four miles from the highway turn right where a sign identifies the road to McNeil Campground and the Ramona Falls Trail. Go downhill 0.6 mile, turn right, cross a bridge and 0.4 mile from the span turn right onto Road S-25D as indicated by a sign pointing to Riley Campground and Horseshoe Trail. One-tenth mile farther keep left at the entrance to the campground and follow the unpaved road 0.5 mile to a sign on your right identifying the Cast Creek Trail No. 773 across the road. Park here.

After several yards pass the wilderness register and climb very steeply in woods then near 0.4 mile begin a series of seven switchbacks. Continue up along the crest at a considerably more moderate grade. You'll even lose some of your hard earned elevation gain during a few downhill segments. Occasionally, you'll have glimpses of Mt. Hood. At 1.5 miles make a short, steep traverse up a north-facing slope then resume a more reasonable grade.

Come to the first good view where you'll be able to see Mounts Hood, St. Helens and Adams and Bald Mountain (No. 8). Make the last steep climb through a narrow corridor of tall, densely packed rhododendrons then near 3.0 miles begin traversing a more open slope of small rhododendrons and scattered trees. East Zigzag Mountain (No. 31) is the peak ahead to the east. Walk gradually uphill, coming to the first of the huckleberry bushes, and then descend 0.2 mile to a saddle and the junction of the Zigzag Mountain Trail No. 775 that reaches the summit of East Zigzag Mountain, a spot with exceptionally far-ranging views, after 0.6 mile and 500 feet of uphill.

Turn right at the saddle and continue down past more huckleberry bushes to the junction of the spur to Cast Lake. If you plan to take the Horseshoe Ridge Trail back, return to this junction after you've visited the lake and follow No. 775 for 0.1 mile to the junction of Trail No. 767. Turn right and begin climbing along the side of Cast Mountain.

To reach Cast Lake turn right and travel along alternating short sections of level, uphill and downhill for 0.6 mile to the lake. To see the beaver dam, continue along the north shore to the outlet creek. The high ridge above to the south is Cast Mountain. If you're backpacking, camp only in the nonvegetated areas of the low bluff above the northeast side of the lake. The tempting sites near the south and west shores are within 100 feet of the shore or are in meadow areas, both places that are too fragile to withstand the repeated compactions of tents and human feet.

Cast Lake

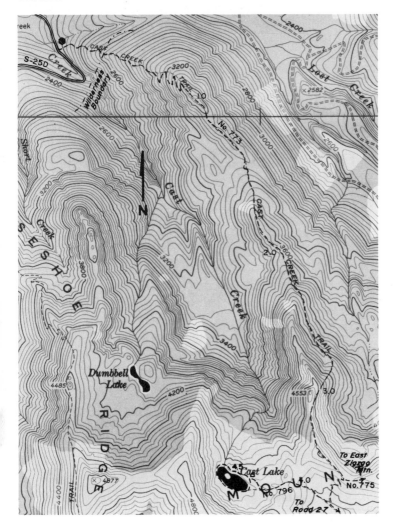

31 BURNT LAKE and EAST ZIGZAG MOUNTAIN

One day trip or backpack
Distance: 4 miles one way
Elevation gain: 2,400 feet
High point: 4,971 feet
Allow 3 hours one way
Usually open late June through October
Topographic map:
U.S.G.S. Government Camp, Oreg.
7.5'   1962

Burnt Lake is one of the best swimming lakes in the Mt. Hood area and the ideal time to try it is from mid- to late-August after a prolonged hot spell. If the conditions have been just right, you'll be able to combine a swim with another delightful feature of the hike; the luscious huckleberries that are especially plentiful around the 3.5 mile point. Even if the swimming and berries aren't at their peak, you'll be able to enjoy the impressive view from the summit of East Zigzag Mountain above Burnt Lake.

Drive on US 26 18 miles east of Sandy or 2.0 miles west of Rhododendron to the community of Zigzag and turn north on the Lolo Pass Road. Proceed 4.0 miles to a sign marking the road to McNeil Campground and Ramona Falls and turn right. Go downhill 0.6 mile, turn right and cross a bridge. One-half mile from the span keep straight and 1.1 miles farther stay right on S-239. Three-tenths mile farther where the pavement ends keep left; after 0.4 mile stay right on S-239G and follow it the final 0.9 mile to the end of the passable road. A sign at the southwest edge of the turnaround identifies the beginning of the hike.

Go through a gate, pass the Wilderness register and boundary and follow the road along the south edge of the clearcut, that is fast growing into a forest. Enter deeper woods and continue gradually up along the road for 0.1 mile to a signed trail on your right. A small log across the road also may mark the junction.

Veer right and meander at a gradual grade through a lovely, lush woods of cedar, Douglas fir, red alder, ferns and smatterings of red and blue huckleberry and rhododendron bushes. Keep right where a path heads back toward the road and continue through the forest to a stream crossing. Just beyond the easy ford begin climbing in eight very steep switchbacks. Drop slightly then climb in three more switchbacks. The tread is level for a short distance then resumes its steep grade. Make two switchbacks, catch a glimpse of Mt. Hood and continue up to a brushy, open area. A considerably more moderately graded trail is scheduled to be built to the west of the present alignment between 1.9 and 2.5 miles.

Walk around the north edge of the clearing to the outlet from Burnt Lake where you may see some crayfish. Cross the creek and climb for 200 yards to the northwest end of the lake. If you're doing the trip as a backpack be sure to camp in developed sites in the woods at least 100 feet from the shore and never pitch a tent in a grassy area. Hike parallel to the northwest shore to the junction of the trail to East Zigzag Mountain.

To reach the summit, keep right, climb briefly and traverse above two ponds. Rise and drop slightly and cross a small stream. Climb, walk through a little clearing and wind up in several short switchbacks to the ridge crest and the junction of a trail (No. 34) to Paradise Park. Turn right and climb more moderately along the crest. Leave the trees at the junction of Trail No. 772 down to Devils Meadow.

Keep right and continue up the grassy summit ridge. Traverse west below the summit then turn right and follow the path up to the site of the former lookout. The main trail descends along the crest to a saddle and the junction of the Cast Creek Trail (No. 30). From the summit you'll be able to see Mt. Hood and Burnt Lake as well as Mounts St. Helens, Rainier and Adams to the north, south to Three Fingered Jack and many landmarks in between such as Bald Mountain (No. 8), Tom Dick Mountain (No. 42), Multorpor and Ski Bowl Ski Areas (see No. 43) and Bonney (No. 49) and Frog Lake (No. 51) Buttes.

Burnt Lake

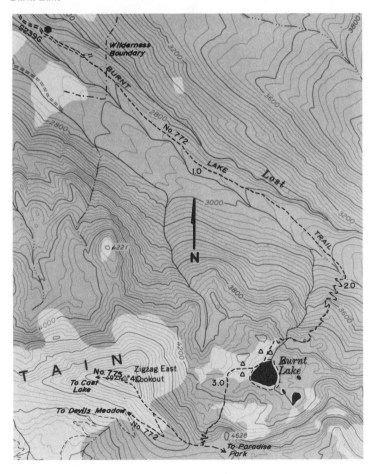

32 RAMONA FALLS LOOP

One day trip
Distance: 5.5 miles round trip
Elevation gain: 700 feet
High point: 3,450 feet
Allow 3 to 3½ hours round trip
Usually open April through November
Topographic map:
  U.S.G.S. Bull Run Lake, Oreg.
  7.5'   1962

For several good reasons, the Ramona Falls Loop is one of the most popular hikes in the Mt. Hood area: the elevation gain is minimal, the grade is gradual, both legs of the loop are scenic in their distinctive ways and 100 foot high Ramona Falls is exceptionally attractive. The hike begins with a photogenic view of the west face of Mt. Hood then follows near the rim of the broad canyon formed by the Sandy River and returns through deep woods beside lovely Ramona Creek.

Proceed on US 26 18 miles east of Sandy or 2.0 miles west of Rhododendron to the community of Zigzag and turn north onto the Lolo Pass Road. Drive 4.0 miles to a sign marking the road to McNeil Campground and Ramona Falls and turn right. Go downhill for 0.6 mile, turn right, cross a bridge and pass the entrance to McNeil Campground. Four-tenths mile from the span keep straight and 1.1 miles farther keep straight (left) again then continue on now unpaved S-25 the final 1.7 miles to the large parking area at the end of the road. The trail begins from the northeast edge of the loop.

Walk several yards across the rocky high water area to a bridge over the Sandy River. It was built high so logs and other debris carried by the river wouldn't collect under the span and eventually destroy the supports, the fate of several predecessors. At the north end of the bridge turn right and climb for a couple hundred feet to a junction. You'll be returning along the trail that continues north from here.

Turn right and climb at a very gradual grade, descending slightly just once. Occasionally, you can see former sections of the old trail that end abruptly where a portion of the slope has slipped. Much of this erosion occurred during the extremely high, violent flow of December, 1964. At 1.8 miles come to the junction of the Pacific Crest Trail (see the Paradise Park to Ramona Falls subsection of No. 41). Keep left, climb gradually for 0.5 mile then descend briefly to the wooded grotto at Ramona Falls.

To complete the loop, cross the creek near the base of the falls on a bridge and after several yards come to a junction. The Pacific Crest Trail veers right here and climbs for 0.8 mile to the spur to extremely scenic Yocum Ridge (No. 33). You could make a longer loop that would add 5.0 miles and 1,550 feet of uphill by continuing along the Pacific Crest Trail to the four-way junction at Bald Mountain and returning to the Ramona Falls Loop along No. 784. Refer to the Ramona Falls to Cairn Basin subsection of No. 41 and to No. 8 for a description of this circuit.

Keep left at the junction of the Pacific Crest Trail just beyond the falls, if you plan to continue the easier loop, and descend for 150 yards to a footbridge across Ramona Creek. Walk downhill through scenic woods parallel to the stream and below a 100 foot high wall of fractured rock. Near 4.1 miles veer away from the creek and farther on come to the junction of Trail No. 784 to Bald Mountain. Turn left, cross Ramona Creek for the last time and come to the junction just north of the high bridge.

Ramona Creek

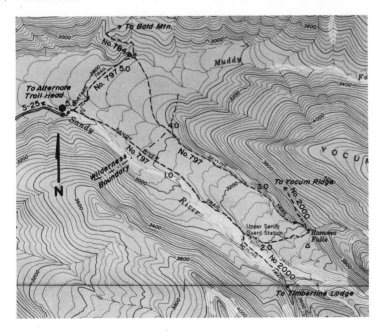

33 YOCUM RIDGE

One day trip or backpack
Distance: 7.6 miles one way
Elevation gain: 3,500 feet
High point: 6,200 feet
Allow 3½ to 4½ hours one way
Usually open late July through October
Topographic maps:
  U.S.G.S. Bull Run Lake, Oreg.
  7.5'   1962
  U.S.G.S. Cathedral Ridge, Oreg.
  7.5'   1962

A few hikes in the Mt. Hood area may equal the scenery enjoyed along the climb of Yocum Ridge but none can surpass it. If the weather is marginal consider doing another trip and save Yocum Ridge for a perfect day. Dominating the view is the west face of Mt. Hood and on a warm, sunny afternoon you probably will hear, and perhaps see, the awesome, momentarily terrifying, sound of a crumbling ice block on one of several nearby glaciers.

Drive on US 26 18 miles east of Sandy or 2.0 miles west of Rhododendron to the community of Zigzag and turn north on the Lolo Pass Road. Travel 4.0 miles to a sign marking the road to McNeil Campground and Ramona Falls and turn right. Go downhill 0.6 mile, turn right, cross a bridge and pass the entrance to McNeil Campground. Follow S-25 1.5 miles, keep straight (left) then continue on now un-paved S-25 the final 1.7 miles to the large parking area at the end of the road. The trail begins from the northeast edge of the loop.

Walk several yards across the rocky high water area to a bridge over the Sandy River. At the north end of the span turn right and climb to a junction. If you make the loop back from Ramona Falls (see No. 32) you'll be returning along the trail that continues north from here.

Turn right and climb at a very gradual grade, descending slightly once, to the junction of the Pacific Crest Trail at 1.8 miles (see the second subsection of No. 41). Keep left, climb gradual-ly for 0.5 mile then descend briefly to the wood-ed grotto at lovely Ramona Falls. Cross the creek near the base of the falls on a bridge and after several yards come to the resumption of Trail No. 797. If you plan to make the loop beside Ramona Creek mentioned earlier, follow the route down to your left after you visit Yocum Ridge.

Keep right on the Pacific Crest Trail and traverse up the wooded slope for 0.8 mile. Switchback right and come to the junction of the spur to Yocum Ridge. (See the third subsec-tion of No. 41 for a description of the route of No. 2000.)

Turn right onto No. 771 and traverse the south side of the ridge for 1.0 mile then switch-back left. After 0.3 mile wind up to near the crest of the ridge then resume traversing. At 5.5 miles pass above a scree area and switchback left. Climb a short distance to a large pond and a well-framed scene of Mt. Hood. Curve around the north side of the pond and climb 0.3 mile to a stream, a good place for a snack stop and the last dependable source of water.

Turn left at the stream—do not cross it—and wind up through attractive woods. Come to a view of Mounts St. Helens and Adams then switchback and pass a view of Mt. Hood. Cross to the southwest side of the ridge and traverse along the frequently grassy slope. Eventually, you'll be able to see Paradise Park (No. 38) on the mountain's southwestern flank just above timberline and pinnacle-topped Mt. Jefferson to the south. Continue traversing to a view-point at the edge of the deep canyon below the ice fall of Reid Glacier. The trail switchbacks and climbs a grassy slope for 0.4 mile to the final viewpoint.

Reid Glacier icefall

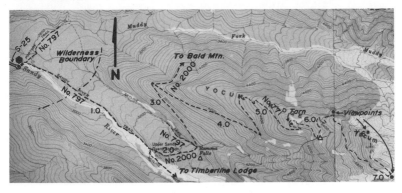

34 DEVILS MEADOW and PARADISE PARK

One day trip or backpack
Distance: 9 miles one way
Elevation gain: 2,880 feet; loss 380 feet
High point: 5,800 feet
Allow 5 to 6 hours one way
Usually open mid-July through October
Topographic maps:
   U.S.G.S. Government Camp, Oreg.
   7.5'   1962
   U.S.G.S. Mt. Hood South, Oreg.
   7.5'   1962

The entire hike to Paradise Park makes a long day but if you'd like a shorter trip two return loops are possible from the summit of East Zigzag Mountain at 4.4 miles. Since several routes go to Paradise Park, you also can take a different trail back from there if you want to establish a car shuttle (see No's 38, 39 and the Timberline Lodge to Paradise Park subsection of No. 41). Regardless of what route you take, though, be sure to allow extra time if you do the hike from late August through mid-September because the huckleberry bushes between 2.5 and 6.0 miles are some of the best in the northern Oregon Cascades.

Proceed on US 26 1.4 miles east of Rhododendron or 7.6 miles west of Government Camp to 27 Road on the north. Turn onto it, after 0.6 mile come to a junction and turn left. Road S-27 is narrow and rough but passable to vehicles without trailers, although a few short stretches of potential quagmires could be problems after prolonged, heavy rains or early in the season. Follow S-27 for 4.3 miles

to where it has been blocked. Trail No. 789 to West Zigzag Mountain that you pass on your left 60 yards from the turnaround is the one you'd be returning along if you make the longer of the two possible loops back from East Zigzag Mountain.

Walk up the closed road for 2.0 miles to its end at Devils Meadow and look up to your left (northwest) for a sign indicating the beginning of the Burnt Lake Trail No. 772. Climb gradually through woods and open areas for 0.5 mile to the junction of Trail No. 767. You'll be returning along it if you make the shorter loop. Keep right, wind up in a few short switchbacks and cross a meadow. Switchback once more up to the crest of a narrow, open ridge where you'll have a good view of Mt. Hood and Burnt Lake.

If you want to make either of the two loops from East Zigzag Mountain, turn left and climb the treeless crest. Traverse just below the summit of East Zigzag Mountain that affords views from Mt. Rainier south to Three Fingered Jack and then descend along the crest to a saddle and the junction of the Cast Creek Trail (No. 30). Keep left and continue down to the junction of the 0.6 mile spur to Cast Lake. Keep left again and continue gradually descending to Trail No. 775 that connects with the Horseshoe Ridge Trail (No. 29). If you want to return along West Zigzag Mountain to Trail No. 789 to the parking area, turn right here and follow the descriptions given in No's 29 and 28. To reach Devils Meadow keep left at the junction of Trail No. 775 and continue down in switchbacks on the Devils Tie Trail No. 767 to the junction with No. 772 that you followed up.

To reach Paradise Park, turn right at the junction on the crest at 3.9 miles, walk on the level into woods and descend to the junction of the trail down to Burnt Lake (No. 31). Keep right, resume climbing and eventually travel through more open terrain. At 5.1 miles come to another good viewpoint. Wind down the narrow ridge, keeping left where a side path heads right, then hike along a saddle. Begin climbing through deep woods, cross Lady Creek at 7.0 miles then travel on the level to the junction with Trail No. 778 (No. 38). Turn left and climb 0.2 mile to No. 2000 that by-passes Paradise Park. Keep straight and continue up 0.4 mile to No. 757. Turn left, traverse 0.2 mile, go in and out of small Lost Creek Canyon and come to the stone shelter below Paradise Park. Refer to No. 38 and the first two subsections of No. 41 for a more detailed description of the area.

Hikers at Paradise Park

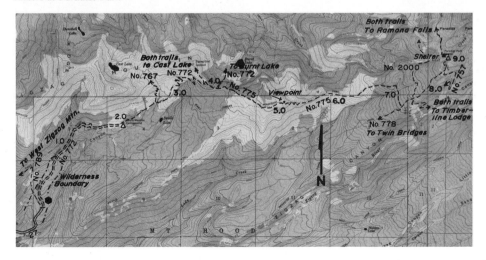

35 FLAG MOUNTAIN

One-half day trip
Distance: 2.1 miles one way
Elevation gain: 800 feet; loss 200 feet
High point: 2,540 feet
Allow 1 to 1½ hours one way
Usually open March through December
Topographic map:
    U.S.G.S. Rhododendron, Oreg.
    7.5'   1962

Flag Mountain is a 2.0 mile long, wooded ridge paralleling US 26 just southeast of Rhododendron. The trail that climbs and descends along its crest affords views of Mt. Hood, Castle Canyon (No. 27) and other landmarks in the immediate area. Rhododendron bushes are plentiful along most of the route so the trip is more attractive during their blooming period from late May through late June. Since the trail ends at a road you could establish a car shuttle and do the hike one way only. Carry water as none is available along the route.

Drive on US 26 to the east end of Rhododendron and turn south on 20 Road, also called Vine Maple Road. After 0.1 mile cross a bridge over the Zigzag River and continue 0.7 mile on 20 Road to a sign marking Road 20E on your left. Turn left and go 150 feet to a sign identifying the beginning of the Flag Mountain Trail. Parking spaces for a few cars are available here. If you're establishing a car shuttle, continue east of Rhododendron on US 26 2.9 miles to 32 Road (Bruin Run) and turn south. After 0.1 mile keep straight on S-32A and follow it 1.1 miles, keeping right where a spur heads downslope after 0.6 mile, to a sign above the road on your right identifying the south end of the Flag Mountain Trail. Road S-32A ends 100 yards farther.

Climb above some summer homes at a moderately steep grade for several hundred yards then switchback a few times and come to the crest of the ridge. Continue uphill at a steep angle then at 0.6 mile begin hiking at a gradual grade. During the walk along the gentle summit ridge you'll have many views of the southwest side of Mt. Hood. The woods become denser and the trail begins a series of short, alternating drops and rises before the final 0.3 mile descent to Road S-32A.

Hunchback Ridge from Flag Mountain trailhead

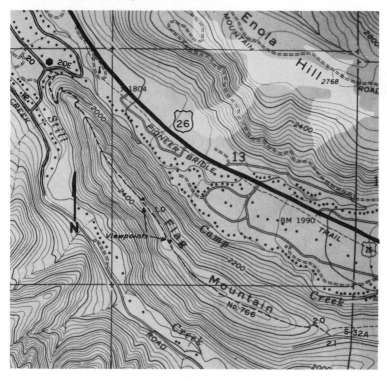

36 DEVILS PEAK

One day trip
Distance: 4.1 miles one way
Elevation gain: 3,210 feet
High point: 5,045 feet
Allow 3 to 3½ hours one way
Usually open late June through mid-November
Topographic maps:
    U.S.G.S. Government Camp, Oreg.
    7.5'   1962
    U.S.G.S. Rhododendron, Oreg.
    7.5'   1962

Very few of the dozens of lookouts that once perched on highpoints throughout the Mt. Hood National Forest still are standing and only two of these are accessible exclusively by trail, the tower atop Bull of the Woods (No. 56) and the one on Devils Peak. Typical of such sites, the view is far-ranging and includes Mounts St. Helens, Rainier, and Adams to the north, Mt. Hood closeby to the northeast and the Salmon River drainage, Salmon Butte (No. 25), Mt. Jefferson and Three Fingered Jack to the south. After mid-summer start the hike with adequate water in case the stream at 1.8 miles is not flowing.

You can do the trip as a long one way hike by following the Hunchback Mountain Trail (No. 23) to Zigzag. This route would involve 6.0 additional miles, 750 feet of extra climbing and a short car shuttle. Conversely, you could use a long car shuttle to half the distance of the return trip by following the scenic trail that heads southeast from the peak and ends at Road S-32 above Kinzel Lake. This route is especially attractive in late June when the wildflowers are blooming.

Proceed on US 26 19.5 miles east of Sandy or 0.3 mile west of Rhododendron to 10 Road and turn south on it. Follow 10 Road (that eventually becomes 12 Road) 3.2 miles, keeping right at junctions 0.3 and 1.4 miles from the highway, to a sign on your right identifying the beginning of the Cool Creek Trail. The last 0.5 mile is unpaved. You also can reach the trailhead by following 20 Road at the east end of Rhododendron for 1.0 mile to the junction with 12 Road. Turn left and continue 1.8 miles to the trailhead. If you plan to establish the long car shuttle, follow the driving directions for Trail No. 44. Continue along Road S-32 beyond this trailhead 5.3 miles to the end of the road, keeping right at the steep spur down to Kinzel Lake.

Climb at a sometimes steep grade for several hundred feet then begin winding up the slope until reaching the ridge top. Walk along the crest for a short distance then traverse a north facing slope. Make a set of very short switchbacks and pass an open spot where you have a good view of Mt. Hood. For the next 0.8 mile follow a course of short switchbacks and traverses then curve into a large, wooded basin. Go in and out of a small side canyon and at a second one cross a stream, the only source of water. Two-tenths mile farther switchback left and climb along the slope then begin a series of several short switchbacks.

Continue climbing through woods then at 2.9 miles traverse to a saddle on the narrow ridge crest. Resume climbing and as you gain elevation pass a few rocky, open areas that afford good views to the east then traverse on the west side just below the rim of the ridge's precipitous east face. At 3.9 miles pass a helispot at a saddle and climb steeply for a short distance to the unsigned junction of the trail to Road S-32.

Turn right and traverse through woods 75 yards to a sign pointing left to Devils Peak Lookout. If you make the loop back along Hunchback Mountain you'll be following the main trail that goes right here. To reach the summit, turn left and after a few hundred feet come to the lookout.

The trail to S-32 traverses the open east slope of Devils Peak then switchbacks down twice. Travel near a narrow, rocky crest, climb then walk at a gradual grade to the end of the road.

Devils Peak lookout

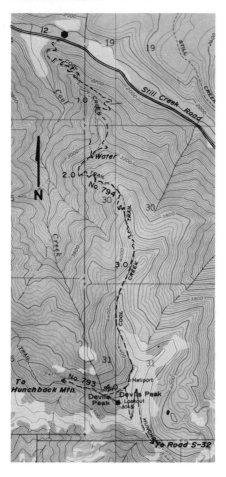

Beargrass

37 PIONEER BRIDLE TRAIL

One day trip
Distance: 4 miles one way
Elevation gain: 1,260 feet
High point: 3,630 feet
Allow 2 to 2½ hours one way
Usually open mid-May through mid-November
Topographic map:
  U.S.G.S. Government Camp, Oreg.
  7.5'   1962

The Pioneer Bridle Trail that generally parallels US 26 for 8.0 miles east of Rhododendron was built by Civilian Conservation Corps crews in 1935. The westerly portion of the route travels on the level between the highway and summer homes but the final half as described below visits considerably more varied and interesting features: an abandoned mine shaft, a tunnel under the old Mt. Hood highway, Little Zigzag Canyon and a portion of the Barlow Road. Since the hike ends at a road, you can do the trip one way only.

Drive on US 26 4.1 miles east of Rhododendron or 5.0 miles west of Government Camp to a large sign pointing north to Mt. Hood Kiwanis Camp at the junction of Road S-354. Park your car in the large turnout on the north side of the highway just east of the junction. If you're using a car shuttle, continue on US 26 for 3.8 miles to Road S-389 on the north side of the highway across from the west end of the loop to the Ski Bowl. Turn north and drive a few hundred yards to a small turnout on your right.

The start of the lower, west end of the hike is near a sign identifying the location of a buried cable. Walk into the strip of woods from here along a faint path and after several yards meet a well-defined trail marked by a sign stating Route of Barlow Road. Turn right and walk on the level between US 26 and Road S-354. Rhododendron bushes are plentiful here and they usually bloom in early June. Begin climbing and make five short switchbacks then come to the more open area of a very old burn. Traverse above US 26 along a slope that has a ground cover of manzanita bushes, not a common plant in the northern Oregon Cascades.

Reenter deeper woods and at 1.3 miles walk on the level across a saddle then follow an erratic grade of uphill, downhill and level. Travel above the highway again then traverse a scree slope and a short distance farther pass the vertical mine shaft on your left. Begin descending and a few hundred feet beyond the digging come to an unsigned spur to the right that reaches the highway after 250 feet.

Keep left and continue gradually downhill. Travel along a scree slope below US 26 and have a view of Mt. Hood then walk through a corridor of rhododendrons. The path on your left goes to private property. Pass a charming old retaining wall and go through the pedestrian tunnel under a section of the former highway. At the far end turn left and walk up a gully for several yards then curve left to a dirt road.

You can follow the dirt road but a more interesting route is to go up Little Zigzag Canyon. Descend to the old highway, turn right and walk the road to the north side of the Little Zigzag River. Turn right and follow a path into the woods. Hike beside the stream and where you come to the base of a falls look upslope to the left several yards for a better trail traversing above you and climb to it. Continue beyond the top of the falls a short distance, cross the stream on poles and climb to the dirt road you could have followed directly up from the highway.

Turn left and wind up along the road. (If you take the road on the return instead of Little Zigzag Canyon, keep left where a connector heads right to a power line access road. However, if you inadvertently end up on the latter, you can follow it down to the old highway.) Where you come to a fork keep left. The spur to the right soon meets another section of the old highway. Continue uphill along the wide trail. Cross a small stream and farther on recross it. Just beyond the second ford switchback right and a couple hundred feet farther curve left and continue gradually uphill the final 0.2 mile, passing a spur to Enid Lake on your left where the route comes close to S-389.

Conie

Rhododendron blossom

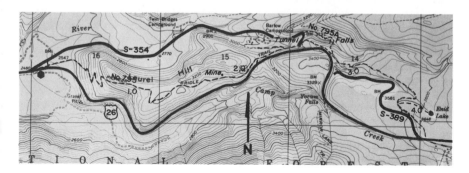

38 PARADISE PARK TRAIL

One day trip or backpack
Distance: 5.6 miles one way
Elevation gain: 3,000 feet
High point: 5,800 feet
Allow 3½ to 4 hours one way
Usually open mid-July through October
Topographic maps:
  U.S.G.S. Government Camp, Oreg.
  7.5'   1962
  U.S.G.S. Mt. Hood South, Oreg.
  7.5'   1962

Paradise Park is an expanse of grassy slopes just above timberline on the southwestern side of Mt. Hood. The area is as lovely in summer with wildflower blooms scattered over the slopes of green as it is during early fall when the golden grass and the red splashes of huckleberry bushes nestled against the grey rocks create a subtle combination of colors.

If you would like to enjoy more of the exceptionally scenic terrain near Paradise Park you could make a 2.0 mile loop that heads north from the shelter below the Park to the junction of a by-pass that goes south to the route you

followed up. Because several trails go to Paradise Park, you can return a different way by establishing a car shuttle. You could: take the Pacific Crest Trail east to Timberline Lodge (see the first subsection of No. 41) or west to Ramona Falls (see the second subsection of No. 41 and No. 32); follow Trail No. 775 to Devils Meadow (No. 34); take the Hidden Lake Trail (No. 39). Water is available at 3.8 miles and just before the shelter.

Proceed on US 26 4.1 miles east of Rhododendron or 5.0 miles west of Government Camp to Road S-354 on the north side of the highway identified by a sign indicating the route to Mt. Hood Kiwanis Camp. Turn north and follow S-354 1.2 miles to a sign stating Paradise Park Trail No. 778 and turn left. Cross a bridge, curve right and after 60 yards come to a sign on your left marking the beginning of the trail.

Walk on the level a couple hundred feet then switchback up to the left. Curve right at the top of the slope and climb at a very moderate grade. At 0.5 mile switchback left and traverse for another 0.5 mile then curve right and travel through deeper woods. Switchback three times and begin the 3.5 mile climb along the ridge to the west of Zigzag Canyon. Near 2.3 miles come near the edge of a bluff above the Zigzag River. Step off the trail for a view of Devils Peak (No. 36), Tom Dick Mountain (No. 42), US 26 and the top of the lifts at Ski Bowl and Timberline. After another 0.5 mile begin veering away from the edge. Near 3.2 miles walk through a small open area then reenter woods and 0.6 mile farther pass a stream, the first source of water. Continue uphill and at 4.5 miles come to the junction of Trail No. 775 from Devils Meadow.

Keep straight (right) and climb somewhat more steeply for 0.2 mile to the junction of the section of the Pacific Crest Trail that by-passes Paradise Park. Keep straight and wind up 0.4 mile to the Paradise Loop Trail No. 757, the original alignment of the route to Paradise Park. Turn left and traverse along the tree-dotted slope of grass and flowers for 0.2 mile. Drop slightly into the small canyon formed by Lost Creek then climb the opposite wall for a few hundred feet to the stone shelter.

To make the short, scenic loop, continue north from the shelter on Trail No. 757 for 0.7 mile then begin descending and come to the junction of No. 2000. Turn left and follow it to the intersection with the trail you followed up. You also could hike east along Trail No. 757 to the other end of the by-pass.

Zigzag Canyon from the air

Shelter at Paradise Park

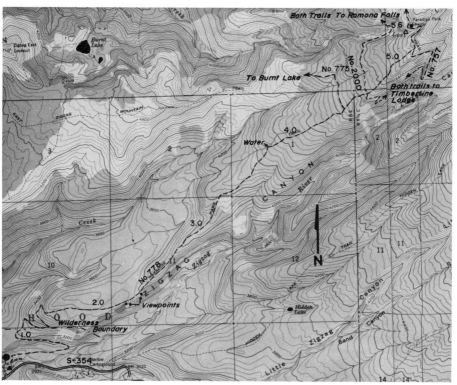

39 HIDDEN LAKE TRAIL

One day trip or backpack
Distance: 5 miles one way
Elevation gain: 2,850 feet
High point: 5,850 feet
Allow 3 to 3½ hours one way
Usually open mid-July through October
Topographic maps:
  U.S.G.S. Government Camp, Oreg.
  7.5'   1962
  U.S.G.S. Mt. Hood South, Oreg.
  7.5'   1962

The Hidden Lake Trail climbs the length of the wooded ridge separating Zigzag and Little Zigzag Canyons and meets the Pacific Crest Trail 1.5 miles west of Timberline Lodge and 3.5 miles east of Paradise Park. You can make a long, strenuous loop by combining the Hidden Lake and Paradise Park (No. 38) Trails. The middle portion of this circuit follows the scenic route of the Timberline Trail for 3.3 miles and includes the hike in and out of Zigzag Canyon (see the Timberline Lodge to Paradise Park subsection of No. 41). The loop would add 3.3 miles of hiking and 1,000 feet of uphill and necessitate establishing a short car shuttle or a walk of 0.8 mile along a road. By making a longer car shuttle you could return east along the Pacific Crest Trail (simultaneously the Timberline Trail along this stretch) to Timberline Lodge. The only good source of water along the Hidden Lake Trail is at 2.2 miles.

On US 26, drive 4.1 miles east of Rhododendron or 5.0 miles west of Government Camp to Road S-354 on the north side of the highway marked by a sign indicating the route to Mt. Hood Kiwanis Camp. Turn north and follow S-354 2.0 miles to a large turnout on your left where a sign identifies the beginning of the Hidden Lake Trail.

Immediately begin climbing and soon make several short switchbacks. Beyond a glimpse of Mt. Hood the route straightens out and continues climbing along the wooded, increasingly broad crest at a moderate grade, except for one short steep stretch. Rhododendron bushes are plentiful and during late June and early July their pink blossoms add color to the light green hue of the forest. Drop slightly, travel at a gradual grade then make one switchback and cross a small footbridge. A short distance beyond the span come to the junction of the side path to Hidden Lake. To reach it turn right and walk 200 feet to near the west end.

To resume the hike keep left on the main trail and travel uphill 0.2 mile to an easy stream crossing, the one dependable source of water along the climb. After about 0.1 mile the trail switchbacks and continues up the wooded crest. Near 3.8 miles pass close to the rim of Zigzag Canyon then climb more noticeably and traverse the southeastern slope of a little side canyon before meeting the Pacific Crest Trail No. 2000.

If you plan to return along the Paradise Park Trail turn left and after 0.8 mile make several switchbacks down into Zigzag Canyon. Traverse up the western wall and where you come to the first switchback keep straight (left). After 0.5 mile meet the junction of the Paradise Park Trail (No. 38), turn left and follow No. 778 to its beginning. While making this loop you could visit Paradise Park with little additional mileage or elevation gain. (See No. 38 and the first subsection of No. 41 for a detailed description of the area.)

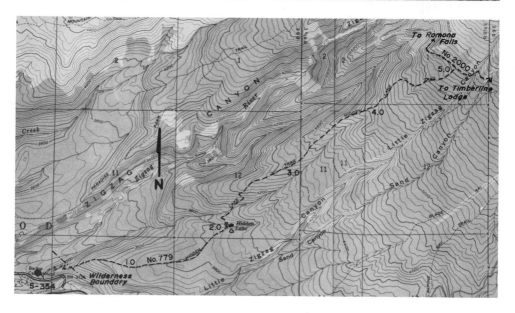

40 ALPINE TRAIL

One day trip
Distance: 3 miles one way
Elevation gain: 2,080 feet
High point: 5,940 feet
Allow 1½ hours one way
Usually open July through October
Topographic map:
  U.S.G.S. Mt. Hood South, Oreg.
  7.5'   1962

Since the Alpine Trail between Government Camp and Timberline Lodge is a popular run for cross-country and downhill skiers, you can check the slopes on the hike for ski pole baskets and other loot from the previous winter. Wild strawberries thrive along the first part of the hike and ripen in mid-summer. However if you prefer the considerably-easier-to-pick huckleberries, you'll want to make the trip around the end of August when they are ripe. By establishing a car shuttle you could have a scenic one way trip by heading east from

Timberline Lodge along the Pacific Crest Trail to Barlow Pass (No. 46). This extension would add 2.6 miles but involve no extra elevation gain. Carry water as none is available along the Alpine Trail until Timberline Lodge.

Proceed on US 26 to the east end of the business loop through Government Camp and turn into the large parking area for the Summit Ski Area and Rest Area.

Climb along the open slope of the ski area, paralleling the east side of the poma lift, then curve right and continue rising to the top end of the upper rope tow where a Motor Vehicle Closure sign on a tree marks the beginning of the trail. Hike along a two track road that eventually narrows into a trail and come to the first of the huckleberries. Near 0.9 mile briefly pass near the West Leg Road that you won't be seeing again until 2.5 miles. It was built in 1931 to replace the original wagon road to the Camp Blossom area. Three years later, instead of widening the West Leg Road, East Leg Road was constructed so a one way loop from Government Camp to Timberline was possible. In the late 1940's the present Timberline Road replaced both.

The grade increases considerably as the trail climbs Big Mazama Hill that is densely vegetated with the tall stalks, and during late June the bulbous white blooms, of beargrass. At the top of the clearing begin rising more moderately along the crest of the broad ridge. Purple lupine and the creamy white petals of the Mariposa lily are two more of the wildflowers you'll enjoy along the climb. If you turn around you can look across the valley to the Multorpor and Ski Bowl Ski Areas (see No. 43) and beyond to Trillium Lake, Olallie Butte (No. 60) and Mt. Jefferson.

Near 2.3 miles pass above a small ravine on your right known as Corkscrew Canyon by skiers. Continue to its head then cross on a fill and follow an old road bed. After several hundred feet where you glimpse the West Leg Road below on your right, veer left and climb in a northeasterly direction. This should be your last view of the West Leg Road.

Follow the route of least resistance, still heading northeast, up the steep, grassy slopes until you come to the Pucci Lift and follow it up to the west end of Timberline Lodge. The building was a Works Progress Administration project and was constructed in the incredibly short time of 21 months between 1936 and 1937. The east wing, obviously a recent addition, actually was included in the original architectural plans for the lodge.

Tom Dick Mountain from the Alpine Trail

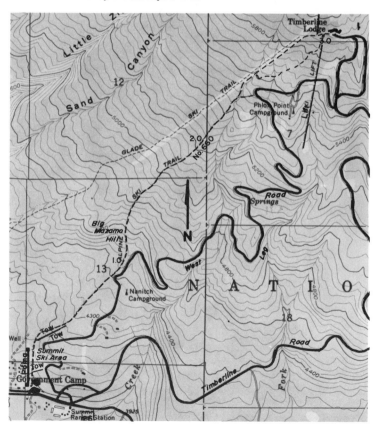

41 TIMBERLINE TRAIL

Backpack
Distance: 37.6 miles round trip
Elevation gain: 9,800 feet
High point: 7,350 feet
Allow 3 to 5 days round trip
Usually open mid-July through mid-October
Topographic maps:
    U.S.G.S. Badger Lake, Oreg.
    7.5'   1962
    U.S.G.S. Bull Run Lake, Oreg.
    7.5'   1962
    U.S.G.S. Cathedral Ridge, Oreg.
    7.5'   1962
    U.S.G.S. Government Camp, Oreg.
    7.5'   1962
    U.S.G.S. Mt. Hood South, Oreg.
    7.5'   1962

In 1892 Will Langille, an early climbing guide on the north side of Mt. Hood, and a companion made the first circuit around the peak on foot. Forty-two years later Civilian Conservation Corps crews began constructing a trail around the mountain. The work was completed in September of 1938 and since then hikers and backpackers have followed the Timberline Trail through some of the most scenic terrain in the Pacific Northwest.

Although the route generally does circle the mountain near timberline, it occasionally drops into deeper woods or climbs to the zone of sparse, ground-hugging vegetation. Most of the many varieties of wildflowers along the trail reach full bloom during the first part of August, though the circuit always is exceptionally scenic. On most sections of the Timberline Trail the glaciated faces of Mt. Hood dominate the scene but frequently the view extends as far north as Mt. Rainier or south to Mt. Jefferson and even the Three Sisters.

If the snowfall on the mountain has been exceptionally heavy, the date the route is open may be delayed several weeks. Early in the season be careful crossing any snow-filled gullies as streams may have melted away the underside and you could break through. Through July, fording the streams fed by glaciers — particularly the Muddy Fork, Eliot Creek and the White River — may present some problems. Do not obtain drinking water from the glacial streams as they contain rock flour that may irritate the lining of your intestinal tract. Although water from safe snow-fed streams is plentiful along most sections of the Timberline Trail, it's a good idea to always travel with your bottle at least half full.

Most backpackers start at Timberline Lodge and hike in a clockwise direction but you can begin the loop at any of the other access points or travel the opposite way. The Timberline Trail passes close to roads at Timberline Lodge and Cloud Cap (see No. 14) at 25.2 miles but the other accesses are along side trails (No's 8 through 12, 17, 32, 33, 34, 38, 39, 40 and 46 and the 3.0 mile section of the Pacific Crest Trail south from Lolo Pass). These many lateral routes make it possible to do the Timberline Trail in sections if you don't have the time or inclination for a long backpack.

A few hardy joggers have run around Mt. Hood in 9 to 12 hours but most people choose to carry camping equipment and adopt a more leisurely pace. The usual time for a complete circuit with few, if any, side trips is three or four days. However, if you have the time many extremely scenic and interesting excursions off the main route are possible and allowing four nights and five days would provide ample time for investigating most of them.

Drive on US 26 0.5 mile east of Government Camp or 2.5 miles west of the junction of US 26 and Oregon 35 to the road to Timberline Lodge. Turn north and proceed 5.5 miles to the large parking area below the Lodge.

TIMBERLINE LODGE to PARADISE PARK
Distance: 4.7 miles
Elevation gain: 1,100 feet; loss 1,380 feet

Walk to the west end of the Lodge, turn right and go uphill 100 yards to a huge, carved wooden sign that marks the Timberline Trail and lists mileages to many places along the route. For the next 13.4 miles and along the final 1.5 miles of the loop you actually will be following the Pacific Crest Trail No. 2000. For numbering purposes, No. 2000 is assigned to the sections that simultaneously are the Pacific Crest and Timberline Trails. On paper, at least, the Forest Service doesn't consider No. 600, the Timberline Trail, to go entirely around Mt. Hood.

Turn left (west) and traverse gradually downhill near timberline. Pinnacle-topped Mt. Jefferson is the high point on the southern horizon. After 0.7 mile be watching for a foundation and fallen chimney 75 feet below the trail. They're all that remain of Timberline Cabin, built in 1915 and used by skiers and

Mt. Hood from Timberline Lodge

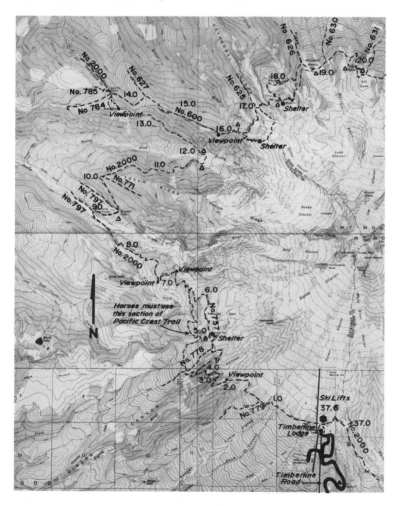

climbers until the early 1950's. A short distance farther traverse in and out of Sand Canyon then just beyond it cross Little Zigzag Canyon. At 1.2 miles keep straight (right) at the junction of the Hidden Lake Trail (No. 39) and begin winding down through deeper woods for a few tenths mile then traverse grassy, open slopes.

At 2.0 miles, where you travel below the crest of a low sandy ridge, leave the trail and climb several yards for an impressive view down into Zigzag Canyon and up to the rock mass of Missippippi Head at the beginning of the canyon. The unusual name for this formation originated in 1905 when the Mississippi delegation to the National Editorial Association conference being held in Portland asked to have Mt. Hood illuminated with fireworks. This site was chosen and subsequently named for the group.

Begin descending in switchbacks to the floor of the canyon, an elevation loss of 950 feet. Ford the Zigzag River and traverse up the opposite wall. Three-tenths mile from the crossing come to a switchback and the junction of a new section of the Pacific Crest Trail, built to enable horse traffic to by-pass the fragile vegetation of Paradise Park. Although this new portion traverses attractive terrain, the best route for foot traffic is along the original trail.

To reach Paradise Park keep right on Trail No. 757 at the switchback and continue climbing along the wooded wall. Switchback once up a sandy, treeless area then traverse the brush covered slopes of a side canyon. Hike along more gentle, grassy terrain and pass the junction of Trail No. 778 from Devils Meadow (No. 34) and Twin Bridges (No. 38). No. 778 descends through clearings and woods and after 0.4 mile crosses the Paradise Park by-pass.

Keep straight (right) and traverse 0.2 mile to the little canyon formed by Lost Creek. Descend to the stream then climb the opposite side to the stone shelter below Paradise Park, the first good choice for a campsite.

When the Timberline Trail was built, five stone shelters (at Paradise Park, Cairn Basin, Elk Cove, Cooper Spur and Gnarl Ridge) and two wooden, three-sided ones (at Ramona Falls and Bald Mountain) were constructed along the route. Both of the wooden structures have been removed in the past few years with no trace of them remaining and only the two stone structures at Paradise Park and Cairn Basin now are entirely serviceable. The stone shelter on the tip of McNeil Point and the wooden one at Elk Meadows, both off the Timberline Trail but

built around the same time as the others, still are in good condition.

If you're by-passing Paradise Park, keep left at the first switchback above the floor of Zigzag Canyon at 3.4 miles. Traverse, make two sets of switchbacks and come to a viewpoint above a slide. Curve right, meet the junction of Trail No. 778 and keep straight. Contour in and out of small side canyons with little streams and waterfalls. At the last and largest canyon you'll have a view of Mt. St. Helens as well as Mt. Hood. Enter deeper woods and descend slightly then cross two small streams and come to the junction of Trail No. 757 from Paradise Park shelter 1.4 miles to the west.

PARADISE PARK to RAMONA FALLS
Distance: 4.5 miles
Elevation gain: 350 feet; loss 2,600 feet

From the shelter below Paradise Park continue north and walk along the base of a high rock bluff. Go through a sandy little canyon then continue along a gentle, treeless slope. Pass a weathered sign pointing to Slide Mountain, begin descending and come to timberline. At 6.3 miles meet the junction of No. 2000 that by-passed Paradise Park, keep right and continue winding downhill. Come to a sign marking the Reid Glacier Viewpoint that also affords a good look at the south side of Yocum Ridge. Continue descending and pass another sign pointing west to Slide Mountain. For the next 9.0 miles you'll be in woods much of the time. This is the only section of the circuit that is below timberline for any great distance.

At 8.8 miles pass above Rushing Water Creek. Although the flat area between the trail and the stream is a tempting place to camp, it actually is not appropriate as there isn't enough space to set up a tent the required 100 feet from the creek. A few hundred feet farther leave the deep woods and come to the broad stream bed of the Sandy River. Ford a clear creek and a few yards more cross the muddy main flow. Follow the obvious path down the sandy stream bed for 0.3 mile then climb the northern bank and come to the junction of Trail No. 797, the southern half of the Ramona Falls Loop (No. 32).

Turn right and climb gradually for 0.5 mile then descend briefly to lovely Ramona Falls. You can camp in the woods away from the trail in the flat area just before you begin the drop to the falls.

Mt. Hood from near Cairn Basin

RAMONA FALLS to CAIRN BASIN
Distance: 7.5 miles
Elevation gain: 2,550 feet; loss 450 feet

Cross Ramona Creek on a bridge near the base of the falls and after several yards come to the junction of another relatively new section of No. 2000. You still can take the lower, original route that is somewhat shorter and avoids the ford of the Muddy Fork. If you decide to do so, keep straight (left) and descend through attractive woods beside Ramona Creek, crossing the stream twice on little footbridges. Two miles from the falls come to the junction of Trail No. 784 (No. 8) where No. 797 curves sharply left, keep straight and pass through a good campsite. Cross the Muddy Fork on a small bridge and begin winding up the northern wall of the valley. At the rim begin traveling at a more moderate grade and after 0.6 mile come to the junction of the newer section of No. 2000 at the former site of the Bald Mountain shelter.

If you want to follow No. 2000 from Ramona Falls, keep right at the junction just beyond the cascade and traverse up the wooded slope at a steady grade for 0.8 mile. Switchback right and come to the junction of the outstandingly scenic trail along Yocum Ridge (No. 33). This section beyond Ramona Falls and the trail that continues along the south side of the ridge were the original route of the Timberline Trail. It was to have climbed above timberline on Yocum Ridge then traversed north along the base of the Sandy Glacier. However, construction of the trail stopped 1.8 miles beyond Ramona Falls when engineers decided it wasn't feasible to build and maintain a trail across slopes that would be covered by snow most of the summer.

Keep left at the junction of No. 771 and traverse mostly downhill along the northern wooded slope of Yocum Ridge for 1.8 miles to the ford of the Muddy Fork. Obviously, the slope along this stretch is prone to slippage. The trail itself was difficult to build and at the beginning of each season maintenance crews have to clear away new rubble. Walk through a brushy area beyond the stream bed, drop slightly then begin climbing in woods. One mile from the crossing the trail traverses the open slope below the summit of Bald Mountain. Curve right and 150 yards before a four-way junction pass an unmarked path on your right to the summit of Bald Mountain (No. 8).

The trail to the left, No. 784, at the four-way junction is the former route of the Pacific Crest Trail and the one you'd have taken if you'd followed the alternate route from Ramona Falls. No. 2000 continues north to Lolo Pass.

Turn right onto the Timberline Trail No. 600 as indicated by the sign pointing to Cairn Basin and Eden Park. Descend slightly then begin climbing moderately and 0.5 mile from the four-way junction keep right at the sign marking the McGee Creek Trail No. 627. When the Timberline Trail was completed the portion of the Bull Run Reserve where entry was restricted extended considerably farther east than the present boundary and trails to the west from the Timberline Trail, such McGee Creek and Cathedral Ridge and the route along the Sandy River, were closed to public travel.

Climb more noticeably to a narrow, wooded crest then continue uphill and cross a treeless portion of Bald Mountain Ridge. As you traverse the grassy slope you'll have fine views of the west face of Mt. Hood, down into the rugged canyon at the head of the Muddy Fork and the north side of Yocum Ridge. (Illogically, the Muddy Fork is fed by the Sandy Glacier and the Sandy River originates from Reid Glacier.) Descend a short distance then begin winding uphill. Where the trail turns sharply right at 16.4 miles a short spur leads to a campsite.

Soon traverse at a more moderate grade, hop a small stream and cross the mossy stones of shallow McGee Creek. Make a few short switchbacks, walk through a grassy area beside a large tarn and pass a second one on your left. Leave the trail and walk around to the west shore for an extremely photogenic view of Mt. Hood. The cover picture for this guide was taken from here in early October. Climb a short distance, go over the crest of a low ridge and come to the junction of the Cathedral Ridge Trail (No. 9) above another tarn. The large body of water to the northwest is Lost Lake (No. 6). Keep right and walk 100 feet to a small stream that runs down the center of a grassy swale, a delightful spot for a snack stop.

If you want to make a side trip to the stone shelter on McNeil Point to the south, turn right at the center of the grassy swale and follow a use-path beside the stream for several hundred yards then climb steeply for 500 feet to a well-worn trail running perpendicular to the valley. This is a section of the original, higher and uncompleted route of the Timberline Trail from Yocum Ridge. Turn right, cross a scree slope, go over a low crest and descend for several yards then curve left. The tread is faint for a short distance but you can see the obvious route

Muddy Fork

traversing the slope ahead. Cross a good sized stream and traverse a rocky stretch to another low crest. Veer right and follow a path gradually downhill for several hundred feet to the shelter. (Refer to No. 9 for a description of some of the landmarks you can see from here.) A use path winds very steeply down from the structure and intersects the Timberline Trail at 15.7 miles.

To continue the trek along the Timberline Trail climb a short distance from the swale and come to a crest identified by a sign as Cathedral Ridge. Keep left at a fork just beyond the marker and descend to the ford of the South Fork of Ladd Creek. The trail climbs a short distance, crosses a little plateau of grass and scattered trees then descends in one switchback to a junction at Cairn Basin. Campsites are available near the stone shelter 100 feet to the right (east).

CAIRN BASIN to CLOUD CAP
Distance: 7.4 miles
Elevation gain: 1,800 feet; loss 1,350 feet

The trail to the left (west) at the junction just west of the Cairn Basin shelter is the former alignment of the Timberline Trail through Eden Park to Wy'east Basin. If you want to follow this route continue downhill along the open slope with a few short switchbacks. Enter woods, curve right and pass through Eden Park to the ford of Ladd Creek. Climb through woods and a few small open areas to the junction of the Vista Ridge Trail No. 626 (No. 10). Turn right and traverse gradually uphill 0.2 mile to Wy'east Basin and the junction of the Timberline Trail.

If you intend to follow the slightly shorter, newer and higher section of No. 600 continue along the trail that passes the north side of the shelter at Cairn Basin and drop slighly to the ford of Ladd Creek. Climb through woods and clearings, cross over a low ridge and traverse downhill along an open slope to Wy'east Basin and the junction of Trail No. 626. An exceptionally scenic side trip from here is the cross-country climb of Barrett Spur (No. 10). Geologists think this massive rock outcropping is the remnant of a volcanic peak that existed long before the formation of the present Mt. Hood.

Cross a small stream just beyond the junc-

tion and continue traversing at a gradual uphill grade. One-tenth mile from Wy'east Basin come to the junction of the Pinnacle Ridge Trail No. 630 that may not be marked. Keep right and 0.4 mile farther pass the 0.3 mile side path on your right that climbs along a grassy swath to Dollar Lake. If you make the trip to this circular tarn continue uphill beyond the lake to the south for a few hundred yards to a viewpoint above Elk Cove.

About 0.1 mile beyond the path to Dollar Lake the Timberline Trail crosses over "99" Ridge. The trail that heads down to the left just before the crest is the previous alignment. Travel downhill, passing through one of the best huckleberry areas along the trip. Depending on the weather conditions, the delicious fruit here ripens from late August to early September. Make one switchback just above the floor of Elk Cove and cross a stream. The stone shelter was located several yards to the east from the trail. By the late 1960's avalanches had reduced it to rubble and the remains were removed a few years ago. The ghostly, weathered trees, their trunks snapped off at the snow line, are further evidence of the force of the avalanches in this basin.

At the north end of the Cove come to the junction of Trail No. 631 (No. 11). If you're planning to camp in the area take this trail a short distance into the woods. DO NOT CAMP in the meadow areas. The Timberline Trail heads east from the junction of No. 631. The route from Cloud Cap to here was a popular use-path by the 1920's so the CCC crews working on this section of the Timberline Trail didn't have to build it from scratch.

Wind down gradually through woods for 0.7 mile to the plank bridge across Coe Creek. Be careful on the opposite bank as the rocks may be slippery. Negotiating the original crossing, 0.5 mile upstream, was considerably more demanding: steel cables were installed to aid in the descent and climb of the steep bank and rockfall usually accompanied the hiker on his way down and up. The new route climbs out of Coe Creek Canyon in irregular switchbacks then traverses at a more gradual grade near timberline. Go in and out of several small side canyons, cross Compass Creek and eventually begin climbing along the wooded western slope of Stranahan Ridge. Go over the crest and decend in and out of additional small side canyons to the plank bridge over Eliot Creek. One-quarter mile farther come to the junction of No. 600A (No. 12) and the campground at Cloud Cap Saddle.

Trail cairn above Cloud Cap

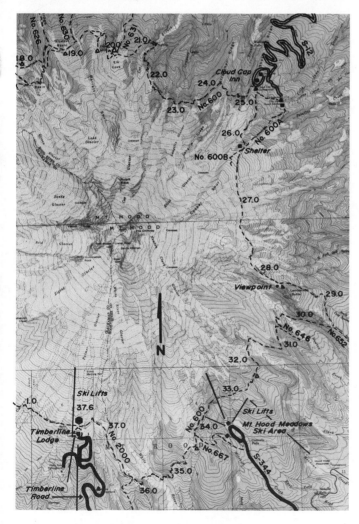

To visit Cloud Cap Inn turn left and walk through the campground to Road S-12. Cross the road and locate a path that heads north up the crest for 200 yards to the old hotel that opened in the late 1880's. It is now closed to the public. Actually, Cloud Cap Inn was not the first resort here. In 1883 David Cooper, an early settler in the Hood River Valley, and two other men built the first road to Cloud Cap. The following year Cooper pitched a cook tent and several sleeping tents in a draw below the site of the present Inn and he acted as climbing guide, his wife operated the resort and Oscar Stranahan, one of the partners in the road, drove the stage.

CLOUD CAP to ELK MEADOWS
Distance: 5.6 miles
Elevation gain: 1,650 feet; loss 2,300 feet

Be sure to fill your bottle at Cloud Cap Saddle Campground as the water sources for the next 4.0 miles aren't dependable. Although you can follow No. 600A through Tilly Jane Campground and rejoin the Timberline Trail at 26.2 miles (see No. 12), the main route is more scenic and direct. Continue south on No. 600 and after a couple hundred yards keep left at the junction of the spur to Eliot Glacier. Hike through woods of thick-trunked alpine firs then come to a moraine at timberline and climb along the slope of sand and boulders. The trail traverses the wall of a small rocky canyon where you may hear, and if you're lucky see, some marmots then curves left and climbs through a swath of stunted white bark pines. Leave the vegetation and travel along a slope of rocks and scattered clumps of grass and other low growing plants. One mile from Cloud Cap Saddle come to the junction of the trail from Tilly Jane Campground on your left and the route up Cooper Spur (No. 14) on your right. From this junction you'll have a good view of Mounts St. Helens, Rainier and Adams and the Upper and Lower Hood River Valleys.

Keep straight and continue above timberline as you travel in and out of side canyons. At 27.4 miles come to the highest point (7,350 feet) of the Timberline Trail. Begin generally descending through more complex terrain then at 28.3 miles come to wind blasted Gnarl Ridge. This impressive viewpoint across from Newton Clark Glacier makes a good rest stop (see No. 17). The route continues gradually downhill along the northern side of Lamberson Butte, passing the ruins of an old stone shelter upslope

from the trail, then curves right and begins winding through deeper woods. Traverse for a short distance, pass through a few small open grassy areas and come to the junction of Trail No. 652 to Elk Meadows. Although reaching the meadows, the largest on Mt. Hood, involves an extra 1.2 miles and 670 feet of elevation loss, the campsites there are especially attractive. If you plan to stay there or just want to visit the meadows refer to Trail No. 17 for a more detailed description of the area.

ELK MEADOWS to TIMBERLINE LODGE
Distance: 9.2 miles
Elevation gain: 2,600 feet; loss 1,820 feet

To complete the loop, traverse gradually downhill to the west along the Timberline Trail from the junction of the route to Elk Meadows at 29.6 miles. Go through a rocky area and cross Newton Creek on a bridge. The route climbs a sparsely wooded slope, curves right and follows the crest of a small ridge that forms the northern side of a little inner valley. Cross its head and climb along the treeless southern wall. Enter woods and curve right around a considerably larger ridge.

Keep right at the junction of the Newton Creek Trail No. 646 and traverse downhill along a large, open sandy slope to the bridge over Clark Creek. After the crossing the route heads upstream a short distance then turns left and begins winding uphill. Cross three streams and continue climbing then round the crest of another ridge. Traverse with brief ups and downs along the slope of large trees and lush, grassy clearings, passing a campsite below the trail at 32.5 miles.

At 33.4 miles come to the Mt. Hood Meadows Ski Area and pass under several chair lifts. Cross a few small streams and come to the junction of Trail No. 667 to Umbrella Falls and Hood River Meadows (No. 19). Keep right and go through a grassy area before entering woods and beginning the winding descent to the broad canyon formed by the White River. Follow stakes across the rocky, sandy bed to a point upstream from the confluence of the two branches. Walk along the bank until you find a suitable place to ford. The established route heads upstream along a bluff then curves left at the edge of the timber. If you have difficulty locating the trail after the ford, aim for the north end of the woods. Climb along the trail for 0.2 mile to the junction with the Pacific Crest Trail (No. 46).

Turn right onto No. 2000 and continue up the open slope of stumps, grass and scattered trees. About 200 yards from the junction the tread stops but tall stakes imbedded in the sandy soil indicate the route. The obvious trail soon resumes and follows the crest of the narrow ridge above White River Canyon. Be careful if you leave the trail as the rim is severely undercut. If you turn around you can see south over Trillium Lake to the Three Sisters beyond Mt. Jefferson. Come to a sign identifying the Buried Forest Overlook. The bleached trunks can be seen protruding from the east wall of the canyon. Geologists think these remains are the result of the latest extensive advance of the White River Glacier. Begin traversing more gradually uphill along the slope of volcanic ash, go in and out of small Salmon River Canyon and walk to the spur that goes down to the east end of Timberline Lodge.

Marmot

42 MIRROR LAKE and TOM DICK MOUNTAIN

One day trip or backpack
Distance: 3.3 miles one way
Elevation gain: 1,715 feet
High point: 5,066 feet
Allow 2½ hours one way
Usually open late June through mid-October
Topographic map:
  U.S.G.S. Government Camp, Oreg.
  7.5'   1962

Mirror Lake, just southwest of Government Camp, is one of the most popular destinations in the Mt. Hood area and even during winter hikers tromp a path through the deep snow to its shore. A lesser used trail continues 2.0 miles farther to the high point of Tom Dick Mountain. In addition to having a bird's-eye view 965 feet down onto Mirror Lake, you'll be able to identify many landmarks, both natural and man-made, on Mt. Hood's south slope only 5.0 miles away.

If you make the hike during late August or early September, carry a container and allow extra time because of the abundance of huckleberry bushes beside the trail between 1.5 and 2.5 miles. This area affords some of the most concentrated picking in the Mt. Hood National Forest.

Drinking water is available from a small spring off a switchback at 0.8 mile. The lake water, as with all such sources, is potable only if chemically treated. Do not obtain water from Camp Creek at the trailhead.

Drive on US 26 7.0 miles east of Rhododendron or 2.0 mile west of Government Camp to a wide shoulder for parking along the south side of the highway.

Cross Camp Creek on a very narrow foot bridge, turn sharply right and walk through woods for several hundred yards to a small span over the outlet from Mirror Lake. Continue uphill through second growth timber of Douglas fir and western red cedar. Pass through a zone of lodgepole pine and rhododendron bushes then near 0.5 mile come to a scree slope that supports one of the densest conie populations in the Mt. Hood area. These adorable, shy little rodents, also known as pikas or rock rabbits, have a distinctive squeaky bleat and, like their considerably larger cousins the marmots, enjoy sunning themselves on rocks. You may see a conie scurrying by with a sprig of a plant or some leaves in its mouth. They collect green matter, spread their harvest to dry then store it in their homes for winter food as they don't hibernate.

Switchback and recross the scree slope then reenter woods. Switchback four more times and come to the junction of the Lake Loop Trail. To continue the hike to Tom Dick Mountain, keep right, soon come near Mirror Lake and pass a sign identifying a campsite area. If you're backpacking, be sure to pitch your tent in the trees at established places and away from the meadow areas around the lake.

At the junction of the other end of the Lake Loop Trail keep right as indicated by the sign pointing to Tom Dick Ridge. Climb gradually then rise at a more noticeable grade along the open slope. You'll be able to see Mt. Hood and farther on you'll have views down the Zigzag River Valley and north to Cast (No. 29) and East Zigzag (No. 31) Mountains, two other very good huckleberry areas. Pass the first of the huckleberry bushes. As you climb higher their density increases and reaches its peak around the 2.0 mile point.

At 2.1 miles come to the crest of the ridge and curve left. Follow along the gradually inclined ridge top through a woods of small lodgepole pines, rhododendrons, beargrass and more huckleberry bushes. Climb more noticeably for the final 0.1 mile to the rocky summit.

The 3.0 mile long east-west oriented crest originally was called Tom, Dick and Harry Mountain but by the 1940's Harry had been dropped. You'll be able to look down onto Government Camp and the Summit Ski Area and see the cuts of the Alpine (No. 40) and Glade Ski Trails. The lift at Multorpor Ski Area (see No. 43) is visible to the east, Devils Peak (No. 36) to the southwest is the highpoint at the eastern end of 6.0 mile long Hunchback Mountain (No. 23) and Mt. Jefferson is on the southern horizon.

Mirror Lake and Tom Dick Mountain

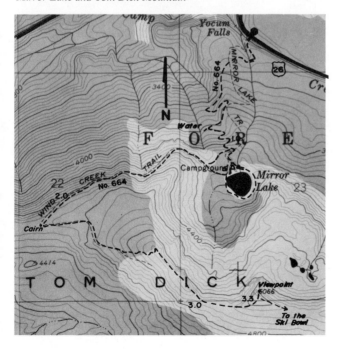

43 WIND LAKE

One day trip or backpack
Distance: 3 miles one way
Elevation gain: 1,030 feet; loss 225 feet
High point: 4,880 feet
Allow 1½ hours one way
Usually open June through mid-October
Topographic map:
  U.S.G.S. Government Camp, Oreg.
  7.5'   1962

The hike to Wind Lake is a varied trip that travels through two ski areas where you can scour the runs for loot lost the previous season and ends at the earliest to warm of the good swimming lakes in the Mt. Hood area. In a normal year, the water temperature should be enjoyable by the first part of July. With just 420 feet of extra uphill and an additional 0.5 mile you can make an easy cross-country climb to the crest of Tom Dick Mountain and peer down on Mirror Lake and Government Camp with the south face of Mt. Hood looming above, north to Mounts St. Helens and Adams and south as far as Mt. Jefferson. If you wanted to establish a short car shuttle you could head west along the crest from Tom Dick Mountain and follow a trail down to Mirror Lake and out to US 26 (see No. 42).

Drive on US 26 29 miles east of Sandy to the business loop through Government Camp and near the center of the community turn south at the sign pointing to Multorpor Ski Area. Go over the highway and continue 0.5 mile to where the road has been closed just before the parking lot for the ski area.

Pass the gate, walk to the west end of the lot, turn left and head up along a road to the day lodge. Turn right and follow the road that heads west at a slight downhill grade toward the main chair lift. The ski area was named for the Multorpor Republican Club whose members created the word by combining the first letters of Multnomah, Portland and Oregon. During the middle part of June the slopes along the first mile are white with wild strawberry blossoms.

Where you reach the bottom of the main lift either stay on the cat road or leave it and follow any of the runs up. The route under the chair is the most direct. Whichever way you chose, eventually come to the upper terminal of the lift and the junction of several roads. Take the one that climbs to the south (left). Traverse, curve sharply left and where the road turns right have a good sighting of Mt. Hood. You'll have extensive views to the south as you follow the road along the south side of the ridge.

At 2.4 miles pass the former site of the terminal for the Upper Ski Bowl lift and continue along the road another couple hundred feet. Where the road curves right and becomes rougher, walk to the left (south) shoulder and head southwest along an old road bed. Descend, losing 225 feet of elevation, for 0.5 mile to a meadow that supports a garden of marsh marigolds in mid-June. Near its center cross a stream that doesn't flow all summer and 120 yards farther come to Wind Lake. Two warnings about alpine swimming: never swim alone and be very cautious about diving into a lake as you can't be sure of its depth or the presence of submerged logs, rocks and twigs.

To reach Tom Dick Mountain, recross the meadow then head up cross-country to the ridge crest. The best view is from an arm of rock jutting north between Mirror Lake and the ponds west of the Ski Bowl. The broken and melted glass is the only evidence a lookout once stood here. The wide swath on Mt. Hood that goes from Government Camp to Timberline Lodge is the route of an aerial tram that operated in the early 1950's. Since skiers could drive up the Timberline Road in half the time the buslike gondola could make the climb, the operation was not successful.

To return to the road you followed up, head east on or near the crest along an old fire trail. Have a glimpse of Wind Lake and 0.5 mile from the viewpoint come to the terminal of the new chair. Walk down a cat road to where you began your descent to Wind Lake and retrace your route.

Wind Lake

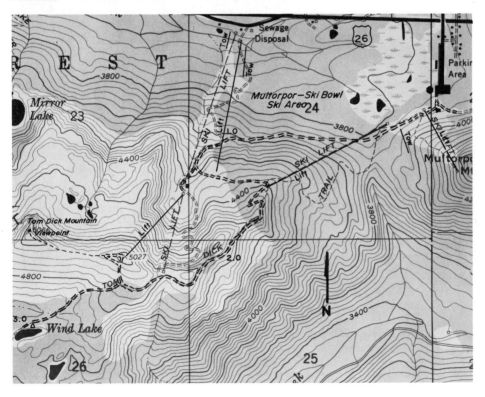

44 VEDA LAKE

One-half day trip
Distance: 1.2 miles one way
Elevation gain: 180 feet; loss 470 feet
High point: 4,690 feet
Allow 30 minutes one way
Usually open late June through mid-October
Topographic maps:
  U.S.G.S. Government Camp, Oreg.
  7.5'   1962
  U.S.G.S. High Rock, Oreg.
  15'   1956

In 1917 two men packed some trout fry to a small lake south of Mt. Hood and a local forester named it for them by combining the first two letters of their names, Vern and Dave. Today, the shore often is lined with fishermen hoping to catch some progeny of those fry. Veda Lake lies in a small, steep-sided bowl and the short climb and descent to it make an ideal family hike. During late August sampling the luscious fruit of the huckleberry bushes beside the trail may slow progress considerably. Start the hike with adequate water as none is available along the trail. The 7.0 mile long Fir Tree Loop (No. 45) starts just across the road from the beginning of the trail to Veda Lake so you could combine the two if you wanted a more strenuous day of hiking.

Proceed on US 26 0.3 mile east of the Timberline Road junction just east of Government Camp or 2.7 miles west of the junction of US 26 and Oregon 35 to a sign on the south side of the road identifying the road to Still Creek Campground. Descend along this road and go through the campground. Seven-tenths mile from the highway begin driving on an unpaved surface and 0.3 mile farther turn right onto Road S-32. Although rough in places, the route is passable and the grade never is severe for the remaining distance to the trailhead. After 0.5 mile come to a four-way junction, keep straight on S-32 and 3.5 miles farther come to Fir Tree Forest Camp. A sign on the right (north) side of the road identifies the trailhead.

Wind up the slope for 0.3 mile then traverse along the face of the ridge through deep woods. Begin descending and at 0.7 mile come to an overlook 350 feet above Veda Lake that also affords a view across to Mt. Hood and Government Camp. This name was given to the site after wagons and other supplies were abandoned there in the fall of 1849 by members of the First US Mounted Rifles. The group had crossed the plains to The Dalles where most of the men were ferried down the Columbia River to Fort Vancouver. The few remaining soldiers were ordered to take the stock and loaded wagons over the newly built Barlow Road to Oregon City before the animals had recouperated fully and nearly two-thirds of them died on the journey.

Switchback left at the viewpoint and wind down the generally open slope that affords more views of the lake. The grade becomes gradual and the route travels north above the shoreline. A trail, that becomes a use-path along the southern side, circles the lake.

Veda Lake

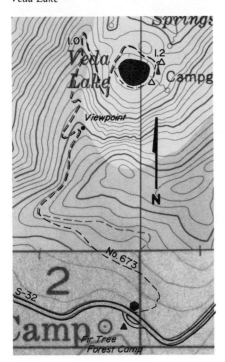

45 FIR TREE LOOP

One day trip
Distance: 7 miles round trip
Elevation gain: 1,650 feet round trip
High point: 4,450 feet
Allow 3 to 3½ hours round trip
Usually open mid-June through October
Topographic map:
  U.S.G.S. High Rock, Oreg.
  15'   1956

This loop actually follows three routes, the Fir Tree, Salmon River and Dry Lakes Trails, and although much of the circuit is through woods, in the occasional open areas, wildflowers, including lupine, rhododendron and the infrequently seen Washington lily, bloom during the early summer. Unlike most hikes, the climbing on this trip is done on the second, instead of the first, half. The three small stream crossings present no problems. The 1.2 mile trail to Veda Lake (No. 44) begins across the road from the start of the Fir Tree Loop so you could do both if you want a little longer outing.

Drive on US 26 0.3 mile east of the Timberline Road junction just east of Government Camp or 2.7 miles west of the junction of US 26 and Oregon 35 to a sign on the south side of the road identifying the road to Still Creek Campground. Descend along this road and go through the campground. Seven-tenths mile from the highway begin driving on an unpaved surface and 0.3 mile farther turn right onto Road S-32. Although rough in places, the route is passable and the grade never is severe for the remaining distance to the trailhead. After 0.5 mile come to a four-way junction, keep straight on S-32 and 3.5 miles farther come to Fir Tree Forest Camp. A sign on the left (south) shoulder of the road about 100 feet west of the Veda Lake trailhead marks the beginning of the Fir Tree Loop.

For the first few hundred feet blue paint has been sprayed on tree trunks to identify the route as it travels through the campground. The trail soon becomes obvious and continues down through woods. Eventually, begin descending at a more gradual grade and at 0.9 mile make an easy ford of an unnamed stream. As the terrain becomes more open you'll be able to see High Rock and Wolf Peak to the south. At 1.2 miles come to the junction of the Dry Lake Trail that you'll be following on the way back.

Keep straight and soon begin winding down through denser, more lush vegetation. Just beyond 2.0 miles traverse above a stream you can hear but not see. Curve sharply left and descend through deep woods to the junction of the Salmon River Trail (No. 26) at 3.0 miles. This route began 10 miles to the west near Zigzag.

Turn left and walk generally on the level with a few slight ups and downs. Cross a small scree area and 0.8 mile from the junction hop the stream you forded earlier. Since you're now about midway along the loop, this is a good spot for a lunch stop. Continue paralleling the Salmon River and eventually begin climbing. At 4.0 mile switchback left, traverse uphill then level off and come to the junction (possibly unsigned) of the Dry Lakes Trail. The Salmon River Trail continues another 1.5 miles before ending at road S-39A.

Turn left and climb at an irregular grade except for one brief descent. One-half mile from the Salmon River Trail cross the unnamed stream for the third time and after another half mile of uphill come to the junction of the Fir Tree Trail you followed earlier. Turn right and retrace your steps to the beginning of the hike.

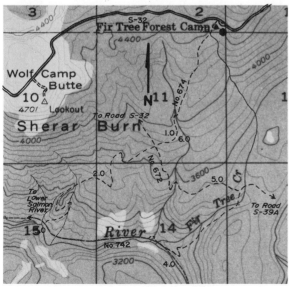

46 PACIFIC CREST TRAIL to TIMBERLINE LODGE

One day trip
Distance: 5.6 miles one way
Elevation gain: 2,000 feet; loss 100 feet
High point: 6,040 feet
Allow 3½ to 4 hours one way
Usually open July through early October
Topographic map:
  U.S.G.S. Mt. Hood South, Oreg.
  7.5'   1962

The Pacific Crest Trail extends from the Canadian to the Mexican border and in Oregon goes from Cascade Locks on the Columbia River along the backbone of the Cascades to south of Crater Lake then veers west to the Siskiyous and continues south into California. Trails described in this guide that follow the Pacific Crest Trail, at least for some of their distance, are No's. 3, 5, 8, 32 through 34, 38, 39, 41, 46, 47, 51, 58, 61 and 62.

The segment of the Pacific Crest Trail No. 2000 that climbs north from Barlow Pass to Timberline Lodge rises through woods to its junction with the Timberline Trail then travels in the open, following the western rim of broad, rocky White River Canyon, before veering west and making an easy ford of the Salmon River. Since both ends of the hike can be reached by road, you could do the trip one way. The one good source of water is at 3.0 miles.

Proceed on Oregon 35 2.2 miles east of its junction with US 26 or about 37 miles south of

Hood River to a sign at mile post 60 identifying Barlow Pass. Turn south here onto Road S-386 and follow it 0.2 mile to a large parking area.

From the southeast edge of the parking area walk several yards into the woods to a large wooden sign marking the Pacific Crest Trail. The section of No. 2000 to the south heads toward Twin Lakes (No. 47) and the route to the east, Trail No. 670, goes to Barlow Butte (No. 48). Turn left, after several yards cross Road S-30 and resume hiking along a trail a short distance to an old section of Oregon 35. Keep right and follow it to the highway. Angle to the right across Oregon 35 to a vehicle closure sign and a Pacific Crest Trail emblem.

Climb for 100 feet into woods, switchback left and after a short distance cross an old cat road. Traverse across a clearcut and at the face of the ridge you can look north at Mt. Hood and southwest to Bird Butte, Eureka Peak, a portion of the Multorpor Ski Area (see No. 43) and East Zigzag Mountain (No. 31) in the distance to the west. Reenter woods, curve to the right around a rocky ridge and traverse uphill at a gentle grade.

Near 2.0 miles cross the Yellow Jacket Ski Trail and pass a clearing on your right. One mile farther come to a campsite off the east side of the tread just before the trail crosses a stream. Traverse above an attractive grassy swath and continue up through woods. At 3.8 miles curve sharply right near the edge of Salmon River Canyon, 0.2 mile farther come to a clearing and beyond it meet the junction of the Timberline Trail (No. 41).

Keep left and continue up the open slope of stumps, grass, bushes and scattered trees. About 200 yards from the junction the tread stops but tall stakes imbedded in the sandy soil mark the route. The obvious tread soon resumes and follows the crest of the narrow ridge above White River Canyon. Be careful if you leave the trail as the rim is severely under cut. Mt. Hood fills the view to the north and if you turn around you can see south over Trillium Lake to Mt. Jefferson and beyond to the Three Sisters. Come to a sign stating *Buried Forest Overlook* and if you study the east wall of the canyon below to your right you can see the bleached trunks. Geologists think these remains are only about 500 years old and resulted from the latest extensive advance of the White River Glacier. At 5.0 miles begin traversing uphill along a slope of volcanic ash, go in and out of a small side canyon and come above Timberline Lodge to the junction of a trail down to the east end of the building.

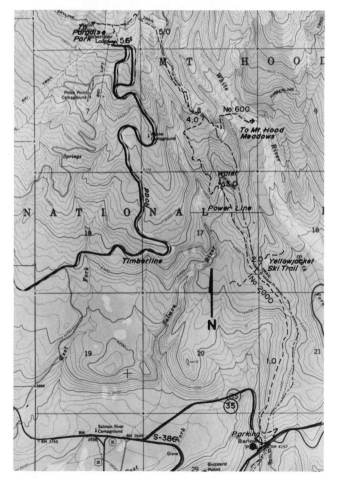

47 TWIN LAKES

One day trip or backpack
Distance: 4 miles one way
Elevation gain: 500 feet; loss 400 feet
High point: 4,500 feet
Allow 2½ to 3 hours one way
Usually open late June through mid-November
Topographic maps:
  U.S.G.S. Mt. Hood South, Oreg.
  7.5'   1962
  U.S.G.S. Mt. Wilson, Oreg.
  15'   1956

After visiting shallow Upper Twin Lake and its lower, deeper and slightly larger counterpart, you can make the first half of the return trip as a scenic loop through a large meadow and to Palmateer Point that affords views of Mt. Hood, Barlow Butte (No. 48) and the broad valley formed by Barlow Creek. This circuit would add no mileage but would involve an extra 480 feet of elevation gain. Since a trail continues south from Lower Twin Lake for 1.5 miles to US 26, you could set up a car shuttle and do the trip one way (see No. 51). Carry drinking water as no good sources are available along the hike.

Drive on Oregon 35 2.2 miles east of its junction with US 26 or about 37 miles south of Hood River to a sign at mile post 60 identifying Barlow Pass. Turn south here onto Road S-386 and follow it 0.2 mile to a large parking area.

From the southeast edge of the parking area walk several yards into the woods to a large wooden sign marking the Pacific Crest Trail.

The section to the north goes to Timberline Lodge (No. 46) and No. 670 goes to Barlow Butte (No. 48). Turn right and walk gradually up through woods. After 0.5 mile begin climbing more noticeably then travel along an open slope, dropping slightly along one stretch, and come to the junction of Trail No. 482. If you make the recommended loop you'll be returning up this trail. Keep right and travel with gradual ups and downs to the junction of Trail No. 495. You also could make a return loop along No. 2000 that continues south here but the route is not especially scenic.

Turn left and traverse to the junction of a spur, No. 482C, to No. 482. Keep straight (right), climb through woods, make one set of switchbacks and come to Bird Butte Saddle. Drop for a short distance to the northeastern tip of Upper Twin Lake. Walk along the length of the eastern shore, passing several good campsites, and just before reaching the southern end pass a sign on your left marking Trail No. 482. If you make the loop, you'll be following this trail on your return from Lower Twin Lake.

Keep straight and climb slightly to a point where you can look down onto a portion of Lower Twin Lake. Begin descending, switchback and continue downhill to the junction of No. 484 to the lake. Trail No. 495 continues west 0.4 mile to No. 2000.

To take an alternate route back to Upper Twin Lake, continue west on No. 495 about 150 feet from the junction of No. 484 to an unsigned path on your right. Follow it up the wooded ravine to the southern end of the upper lake, curve right and rejoin No. 495.

To make the recommended loop from Upper Twin Lake, climb along No. 482, go over the crest of the ridge and traverse along the east side of the slope. One-half mile from the lake pass a viewpoint just off the trail on the right then begin descending to the junction of No. 482C. Keep straight (right) and continue downhill. Come to an open crest then make a little switchback down to a meadow and small pond. Follow the markers along the eastern edge of the clearing to a sign stating *Viewpoint*. Turn right and traverse up the side of the low slope then curve left and climb along the broad, sparsely vegetated crest to Palmateer Point. To complete the loop, curve north at the junction of the spur to the viewpoint and cross the meadow then begin climbing. Keep left at the junction of Trail No. 482A to Devils Half Acre Meadow and continue climbing to the Pacific Crest Trail.

Meadow below Palmateer Point

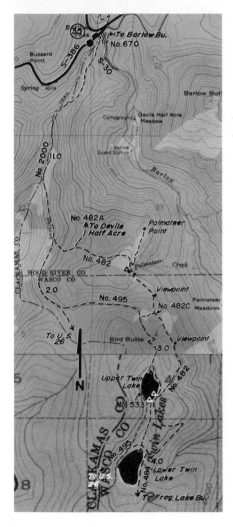

48 BARLOW BUTTE and RIDGE

One day trip
Distance: 3.2 miles one way
Elevation gain: 1,400 feet; loss 520 feet
High point: 5,160 feet
Allow 2 hours one way
Usually open late June through October
Topographic map:
  U.S.G.S. Mt. Hood South, Oreg.
  7.5'   1962

In 1845 Samuel Barlow became the first person to lead a wagon train across the Cascades and naturally several geographic features were named for him. The short side trip to the site of a former lookout on the summit of Barlow Butte is fun even though tall trees now block most of the once extensive view. However, a fine overlook is just a bit farther along the main trail at 1.7 miles. From there you can see Mt. Hood, Bonney Butte (No. 49)—the long flat ridge to the east, Bird and Frog Lake (No. 51) Buttes and south to Olallie Butte (No. 60), Mt. Jefferson and Smith Rocks. If you want a longer hike you can follow the crest of Barlow Ridge to another viewpoint at 3.2 miles. Carry water as the sources along the hike aren't dependable.

Proceed on Oregon 35 2.2 miles east of its junction with US 26 or about 37 miles south of Hood River to a sign at mile post 60 identifying

Barlow Pass. Turn south here onto Road S-386 and follow it 0.2 mile to a large parking area.

From the southeast edge of the parking area walk several yards into the woods to a large wooden sign marking the Pacific Crest Trail. The section to the south heads toward Twin Lakes (No. 47) and the one to the north climbs to Timberline Lodge (No. 46). Keep straight, as indicated by the sign identifying the Barlow Butte Trail No. 670, and descend along a section of the Barlow Road for 100 yards to S-30. Walk down it 100 feet to the resumption of the trail from the east shoulder. Switchback left and continue downhill 0.3 mile to a small meadow where Trail No. 485 goes straight (south) to Devils Half Acre Meadow.

Look left (east) across the clearing for a cross-country ski marker high on a tree and follow the path to it. Travel uphill for 0.2 mile to a small sign identifying the route of Trail No. 670. The path that continues straight (north) ends at an abandoned section of old Oregon 35.

Turn right at the sign and continue gradually uphill. Cross a saddle near the top of a clearcut then wind up in nine very steep switchbacks interrupted by one brief moderate stretch. Travel at a more reasonable grade as you traverse the southeast then the south side of Barlow Butte to a small clearing. The 150 yard long, unmaintained trail to the summit heads up to the left from here. If you take it, be careful not to stumble into the old outhouse pit several yards below the top. To reach the first good viewpoint, follow the main trail as it curves right in the middle of the clearing and descend to the treeless crest.

If you want to hike to the farther viewpoint, continue along or near the crest through woods and clearings, passing several large rock outcroppings. One-half mile from the junction of the short spur to Barlow Butte summit keep right where a horse trail leaves the main route. Climb along the slope and keep right again then travel through deeper woods. Where the trail becomes faint in a flat, open area along the crest look for the resumption of the tread at the southeast (left) edge of the clearing. Farther along at another open area on the ridge top the trail resumes at the right edge. Blazes on trees mark the route where the path is faint. At 2.5 miles begin descending to a sparsely wooded saddle where you can see ahead 50 yards to a rocky outcropping on the crest. Reenter deeper woods and traverse the north side of the slope for a short distance to an unmarked path to the right. Turn right and wind up the path to the summit rocks.

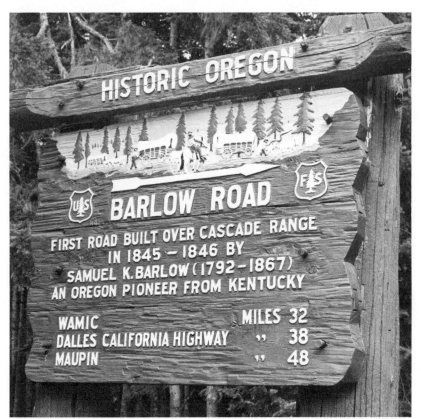

HISTORIC OREGON

BARLOW ROAD

FIRST ROAD BUILT OVER CASCADE RANGE
IN 1845 – 1846 BY
SAMUEL K. BARLOW (1792–1867)
AN OREGON PIONEER FROM KENTUCKY

WAMIC	MILES	32
DALLES CALIFORNIA HIGHWAY	"	38
MAUPIN	"	48

Sign at trailhead

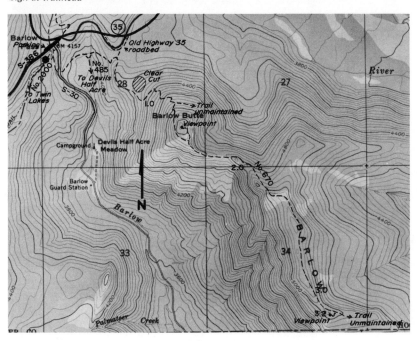

49 BONNEY BUTTE

One day trip
Distance: 2.6 miles one way
Elevation gain: 1,580 feet
High point: 5,480 feet
Allow 1½ hours one way
Usually open late June through October
Topographic maps:
  U.S.G.S. Badger Lake, Oreg.
  7.5'   1962
  U.S.G.S. Mt. Wilson, Oreg.
  15'   1956

If the possibility of sharing your destination with a vehicle doesn't bother you, the climb along the obscure Bonney Meadows Trail affords a chance to visit a part of the Mt. Hood area not so familiar to many hikers. From the treeless summit of Bonney Butte, situated in the vicinity of Barlow (No. 48) and Frog Lake (No. 51) Buttes, the view includes the large expanse of Bonney Meadows below to the east, Mounts Adams and Hood to the north, Mt. Jefferson and Olallie Butte (No. 60) to the south, Smith Rocks and Tygh Valley to the southeast and the Multorpor and Ski Bowl Ski Areas to the west. Carry drinking water as the stream you cross at 1.7 miles is not a good source as it flows through a campground.

Drive on Oregon 35 4.5 miles east of its junction with US 26 or 34.5 miles south of Hood River to the wide, rocky swath of White River

Canyon and at its east side turn south onto paved Road S-408. Follow it 6.6 miles then turn left onto S-346, as indicated by a sign pointing to Rock Creek Reservoir, and proceed 0.9 mile to a four-way junction. Veer left onto S-346A and park along the shoulder just beyond the junction. The trail begins several yards upslope from the *Dead End* sign on S-346A and is marked by a small wooden sign on a tree stating *Trail 471.*

Climb moderately through woods for a few hundred yards then make three switchbacks. Near 0.5 mile pass a sign on your left where a faint, no longer maintained trail climbs east to Swamp Creek and Road S-446. Stay left on the main route and continue traversing up the forested slope. The ground cover along this stretch includes huckleberry bushes and, occasionally, Mt. Hood is visible beyond the curtain of limbs. Near 1.2 miles the woods become more open and you'll be able to see the treeless slope on the south side of Bonney Butte. Travel above Bonney Creek for several hundred yards and come to Road S-338.

Turn left and continue gradually up along the road, passing the edge of lush Bonney Meadows (see No. 50). Keep left at the spur to the campground then 0.3 mile farther turn left onto a road. Walk almost on the level for a few hundred yards then resume climbing to the road's end at the summit. From here you can study White River Canyon and the other landmarks on Mt. Hood's southeastern slope and you may be able to identify Wildcat Mountain (No. 21) and Devils Peak (No. 36) to the west and Bull of the Woods (No. 56) and Battle Ax to the south.

As anyone who has hiked much in the Mt. Hood area has discovered, many highpoints reached by trails are covered with rubble similar to that found on the summit of Bonney Butte. These wads of melted glass, bits of rusted metal and, sometimes, four cement pillars or pieces of lumber are all that remain of the lookouts that once stood there. During the 1960's aerial detection of forest fires became the predominant means of surveillance. As interesting and charming as these obsolete lookouts were, they would have been too costly to maintain and would have become safety hazards as they deteriorated so Forest Service personnel destroyed them. A few lookouts remain in the Mt. Hood National Forest, such as the ones on Devils Peak and Bull of the Woods and elsewhere in the Cascades some still are staffed during the summer, such as those atop Coffin Mountain and Black Butte.

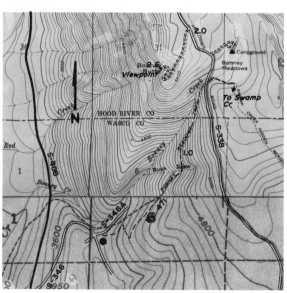

50 BOULDER LAKES

One day trip or backpack
Distance: 2.5 miles one way
Elevation gain: 170 feet; loss 800 feet
High point: 5,250 feet
Allow 1 to 1½ hours one way
Usually open mid-June through October
Topographic map:
  U.S.G.S. Badger Lake, Oreg.
  7.5'   1962

Before or after the short trip to Boulder and Little Boulder Lakes you'll probably want to explore the acres of grassy terrain comprising Bonney Meadows that extends to the south from the beginning of the hike. The many varieties of wildflowers scattered over the meadow are at their best during mid-June. Since the route descends to reach the lakes, you'll do most of the climbing on the return. Begin with a full bottle of water as the lakes are not a good source and Kane Springs is very small.

Proceed on Oregon 35 6.2 miles east of its junction with US 26 or 33 miles south of Hood River to the Bennett Pass Road (S-21) across from the spur to Mt. Hood Meadows Ski Area. Turn south on S-21 and after 4.3 miles along the graveled surface come to the junction of S-338. If you're doing the hike early in the season portions of the road ahead may be blocked by snow. However, the trailhead is only 1.4 miles farther so the extra mileage you would have to hike is not great. Keep right on S-338 and after 1.0 mile continue straight (left) at the junction of the spur to the Bonney Butte (No. 49) helispot. Two-tenths mile farther turn left at the sign marking the road to Bonney Meadows Campground. Go the final 0.2 mile to the beginning of the hike at a sign stating *Boulder Lake Trail* at the north edge of the loop through the campground.

Walk on the level and after several hundred feet come to the northernmost part of Bonney Meadows. (Bonney Butte and Meadows were named for Augustus Bonney, a stockman who settled in the Tygh Valley in 1875.) Cross Bonney Creek and soon enter woods. Hike at a gradual uphill grade then curve left and begin traversing downhill. Switchback right and continue descending. The grade becomes more gradual and the trail crosses a scree slope. Reenter woods and beyond a second rocky area pass a sign at 1.5 miles identifying Kane Springs. Soon curve sharply left and begin dropping at a moderately steep grade above Boulder Lake. The trail passes through a camp area along the eastern shore. This is the best spot along the hike for a lunch stop or to establish a camp. Be sure to camp at least 100 feet from any shoreline.

The trail continues near the shore to the exit creek and the junction of the route past tiny Spinning Lake to a logging road. Keep right (straight) on the main trail and after a short distance begin climbing along a slope. After 0.1 mile of uphill come to a crest. Descend slightly then walk on the level to within sight of shallow, tree-rimmed Little Boulder Lake. The trail tread stops before actually reaching the shore.

Boulder Lake

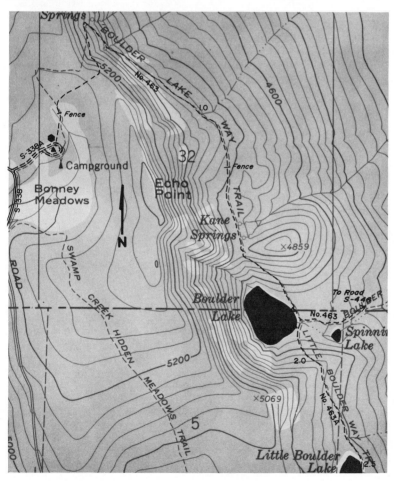

51 FROG LAKE BUTTES LOOP

One day trip
Distance: 5.4 miles round trip
Elevation gain: 1,555 feet; loss 200 feet
High point: 5,293 feet
Allow 3 hours round trip
Usually open late June through October
Topographic map:
  U.S.G.S. Mt. Wilson, Oreg.
  15'   1956

Frog Lake Buttes are less than 2.0 miles south of Lower Twin Lakes and, in fact, you walk along it's shore near the beginning of the loop. If you wanted a side trip you could climb to Upper Twin Lake (No. 47). The special lure of the hike, though, is the extensive view from the large summit area of the more southerly of the two buttes. The south and southeast sides of Mt. Hood fill the view to the north and you can see south to Mt. Jefferson, the Three Sisters and Smith Rocks southeast of Madras. Other landmarks include Silver Star in Washington, Cast Mountain (No. 29), the Ski Bowl Ski Area (see No. 43) and Bird Butte to the north, Bonney Butte (No. 49) and Tygh Valley to the east and Bull of the Woods (No. 56) to the south. Carry water as the trail crosses no streams.

Drive on US 26 5.0 miles south of its junction with Oregon 35 to signs pointing to Frog Lake and Recreation Trail, turn left (east) and go into the large parking area.

The trail begins from the northwest corner of the parking area. After a few hundred feet, come to a cross trail, turn right and pass a sign giving the mileage to Barlow Pass. A short distance farther come to the junction of Trail No. 530 to Frog Lake. Keep left on the Pacific Crest Trail No. 2000 and begin climbing. Switchback once, come to the junction of Trail No. 495 and turn right, as indicated by the sign identifying it as the route to Lower Twin Lake. Descend slightly, curve gradually along the slope and come to the junction of the trail to the lower lake. Trail No. 495 climbs for 0.6 mile to Upper Twin Lake and rejoins the Pacific Crest Trail 1.2 miles farther.

Turn right and go downhill to the northeast shore of the lake. Keep left, following the sign stating *Frog Lake Buttes,* and walk near the shore to the junction of Trail No. 484. Trail No. 532 continues around the lake. Turn left and a few yards farther pass a sign indicating you're on the trail to the Buttes. Traverse up the slope at an erratic, but never severe, grade for 1.2 miles to a saddle and the junction of Trail No. 530. You'll be following this route down if you make the suggested loop.

Keep straight (left) and soon begin climbing, sometimes steeply, for 0.7 mile to a road. Turn left onto it and after several yards veer right and climb briefly to a crest then head northeast across the clearing to a better viewpoint. Or, you can turn right onto the road then veer left at a fork and head toward the viewpoint. Until several years ago a very tall steel fire lookout stood here. No trail goes to the northern butte but it is forested and wouldn't offer good views, anyway.

To make the loop, return to the junction at 3.0 miles and keep left on No. 530. Descend due west, cross the access road to Frog Lake Buttes and continue downhill along the trail to another road. Turn right and follow it a short distance to a trail on your left. Take the path to a third road, turn right and stay on it to the south end of the parking area.

Mt. Hood from Frog Lake Buttes

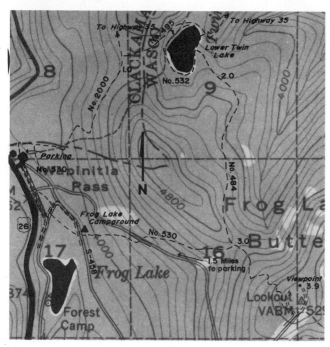

52 DRY RIDGE

One day hike
Distance: 5.7 miles one way
Elevation gain: 3,560 feet
High point: 4,554 feet
Allow 4 hours one way
Usually open June through October
Topographic map:
  U.S.G.S. Fish Creek Mtn., Oreg.
  15'   1956

Some hikes, because of the scenic terrain they traverse or the spectacular views they afford, are best saved for good weather. But trips that travel mostly through woods are enjoyable on sunny, cloudy or even rainy days and, in fact, some woods are more attractive in gloomy conditions. The climb of Dry Ridge is one of these all-weather hikes. If the weather is nice, though, you'll want to make the short cross-country trip to Grouse Point where you'll be able to see the top two-thirds of Mt. Hood and

look into the deep, wide canyon holding the South Fork of the Roaring River.

Early in June iris, not commonly seen in the northern Oregon Cascades, and other wildflowers bloom along the lower elevations of the hike and around the third week in June the many rhododendron bushes beyond the 2.5 mile point add big splashes of pink to the forest green.

From Estacada proceed southeast on Oregon 224, the Upper Clackamas River Road, 18 miles to the entrance to the Roaring River Campground at mile post 42. Turn left (east) and drive through to its north end where a sign identifies the beginning of the Dry Ridge Trail.

After several feet keep right and walk above a pool in the Roaring River. Several yards farther switchback right and come to a power line cut. Follow the swath up to the southeast then reenter woods. Climb at a steady 20 percent grade in nine switchbacks. Travel along the crest of a narrow ridge, make two short switchbacks then traverse at a more gradual angle to a rambunctious stream in a lovely glen, the last source of water along the hike.

Resume climbing a moderately steep grade in seven switchbacks and come to a small scree slope. In 1979 trail crews are scheduled to begin relocating the trail to the north from here. It will follow the edge of the breaks (the place where a slope drops off very steeply) and provide more interesting scenery. This realignment is necessary because the terrain between 3.0 and 5.0 miles currently traversed by the trail is going to be logged. Until this new route is completed, climb a bit farther then walk east away from the rim at a shallow angle in an elegant forest of tall, widely spaced firs. Eventually, the gradient increases. Travel through woods whose composition now has changed to considerably smaller trees and a ground cover of beargrass to a crest at 4.9 miles. The new section of trail will meet the old one here.

To reach the view at Grouse Point, turn right and walk near the rim. Leave the forest, pass through a patch of dense rhododendrons then begin traveling through a more grassy area. Note where you start to veer away from the rim and about 0.2 mile from there in the above noted grassy section turn left and head cross-country several hundred yards to the treeless rim. If you come to two metal signs listing mileages to Cache Meadow (No. 53), Roaring River and Supplement Lookout, you've gone too far. The main trail continues southeast through woods and soon meets the route up from Serene Lake (No. 53).

Along the Roaring River

53 SERENE LAKE-CACHE MEADOW LOOP

One day trip or backpack
Distance: 7.7 miles round trip
Elevation gain: 1,900 feet
High point: 5,000 feet
Allow 4 to 4½ hours round trip
Usually open July through October
Topographic maps:
  U.S.G.S. Fish Creek Mtn., Oreg.
  15'   1956
  U.S.G.S. High Rock, Oreg.
  15'   1956

This moderately long loop offers a variety of places to visit, each quite different in character. Two short spurs go to Middle and Lower Rock Lakes and if you're doing the hike on a warm day from late July through August you may want to swim in either of them or Serene Lake. At 4.7 miles the trail passes a viewpoint where you can look 650 feet down onto Serene Lake and north to Mounts St. Helens, Rainier, Adams and Hood. The route then winds down to the grassy expanse of Cache Meadow. This is an inviting place to rest before completing the hike and the animal life in the stream at the southwest end is fascinating. Except for the easy ford of the South Fork of the Roaring River at 1.0 mile, no potable water is easily available along the hike.

From Estacada drive southeast on Oregon 224, the Upper Clackamas River Road, 26 miles to a junction just beyond Ripplebrook Campground. Turn left onto S-57 and after 8.2 miles keep left on S-58. Continue on S-58, that is unpaved after 5.1 miles, for 5.8 miles to a junction where two roads go left and take the upper one, S-457. After 1.2 miles keep left on S-456 and follow it 4.1 miles to the junction of S-456A. Keep left and after 0.1 mile come to the Frazier Turnaround Campground where a sign marks the beginning of the Serene Lake Trail.

Descend through woods, keeping left on the main trail after a few hundred yards where an unmarked path veer off to the right. At 0.6 mile pass the junction of the 0.2 mile spur to Middle Rock Lake and continue downhill 0.1 mile to the junction of the short path that drops to Lower Rock Lake.

Continue descending on the main trail to the stream crossing at 1.0 mile. Hike near a few small open areas, descend, then travel uphill and traverse along the base of an immense scree slope. Switchback up then round the face of the ridge and traverse along its northwest side before following a meandering course to the north shore of Serene Lake. Continue on the trail, cross the broad, shallow outlet creek and keep left where the trail forks. If camping, be sure to stay at least 100 feet from the shoreline.

Traverse up to the northwest and curve around the face of the ridge. Hike along the lower end of a scree slope then climb in switchbacks to a broad ridge crest and the junction of the trail to Dry Ridge (No. 52). Turn left and climb moderately, keeping left (straight) at the junction of Three Lynx Way. Descend slightly then resume traveling uphill to a large logged area. Continue to the east end of the clearcut and if you want to visit the viewpoint, turn left, leaving the trail, and walk northwest to the rim.

The main trail begins winding downhill at 5.2 miles and comes to the northern end of Cache Meadow where the tread becomes faint. Walk along the left (east) side of the clearing, go through a small strip of trees and continue along the eastern side of the meadow to a shelter in the woods at the edge of the grass. Head east from the shelter and cross a portion of the meadow, keeping a tarn on your left. Enter woods and after several yards keep left where the trail forks and begin climbing for 0.7 mile to an old road. Turn right, climb slightly then descend along the road for 1.5 miles, passing the trail to Shellrock Lake a short distance before reaching the campground.

Cache Meadow

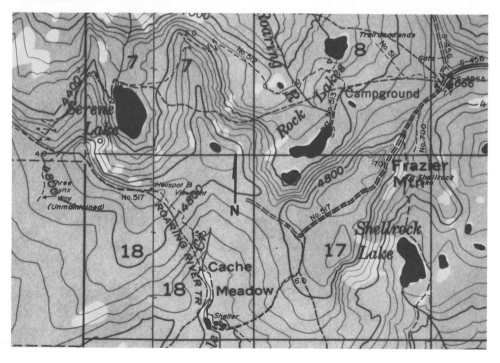

54 FISH CREEK MOUNTAIN

One day trip or backpack
Distance: 2.1 miles one way
Elevation gain: 1,450 feet
High point: 5,098 feet
Allow 1 hour one way
Usually open June through November
Topographic map:
  U.S.G.S. Fish Creek Mtn., Oreg.
  15'   1956

Located southeast of Estacada, Fish Creek Mountain is the westernmost hike in the Clackamas and Collowash River drainages described in this guide. (The others are No's. 52, 53 and 55 through 57.) From the small summit area you'll be able to see Mounts St. Helens, Rainier, Adams and Hood to the north and south to Mt. Jefferson, Olallie Butte (No. 60), Three Fingered Jack and North and Middle Sisters, with an especially good view of the expanse of Collier Glacier on the former. A 0.6 mile spur descends to High Lake, a good destination for a little side trip or a place to camp if you're doing the trip as a short backpack. The Fish Creek Trail is especially attractive during late June when the wildflowers are blooming. Carry water as the route crosses no streams.

From Estacada proceed southeast on Oregon 224, the Upper Clackamas River Road, 22 miles to Sandstone Road, S-53, on your right just before a bridge. Turn right and after 4.0 miles turn right again, still on S-53 that now has a gravel surface. All the junctions are marked by signs pointing to Fish Creek Trail. After another 4.0 miles turn left, staying on S-53, and 1.0 mile farther keep right on S-53C. One mile farther at a saddle keep right on S-505D and continue the final 0.5 mile to the trailhead.

Climb steeply along a rocky slope for several yards to the crest of the narrow ridge. Rise through attractive woods sprinkled with rhododendron bushes. Make two sets of switchbacks on the west side of the ridge then cross over to the east slope. Switchback and return to the west side, travel along the crest then traverse the east slope to a grassy saddle.

Continue along the crest or the east side, still hiking through areas of lush grass. Pass some rock outcroppings and walk along the ridge top past rocks, grass and wildflowers. Drop slightly, resume climbing in deeper woods and switchback to the west side. Descend briefly for a second time and walk at a gradual uphill grade along the broad crest to the junction of the spur down to High Lake.

To reach the summit keep left, climb then drop to a small saddle. Resume climbing, contour around a rocky area and traverse along the northwest facing slope to the open summit. Some lumber and other rubble indicate this once was the site of a fire lookout.

If you intend to visit High Lake, return to the junction at 1.8 miles and descend in three separate sets of switchbacks then wind down to the lake. This side trip involves an elevation loss of 435 feet.

Mt. Jefferson from Fish Creek Mountain

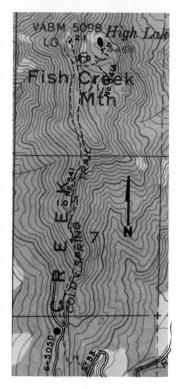

55 BAGBY HOT SPRINGS

One-half day trip
Distance: 1.5 miles one way
Elevation gain: 230 feet
High point: 2,300 feet
Allow 1 hour one way
Usually open April through November
Topographic map:
 U.S.G.S. Battle Ax, Oreg.
 15'   1956

At the end of this short, easy hike through attractive woods to Bagby Hot Springs you can soak in one of the long wooden tubs in the rustic bathhouse. During mid-summer you may not even reach the Springs before wanting to get wet since at 1.2 miles the route crosses Hot Springs Fork that has many inviting pools.

If you would like a longer trip you can continue south along the main trail that passes Silver King Lake after 8.0 miles then visits Twin Lakes before ending at Elk Lake 11 miles from the Hot Springs.

Drive southeast from Estacada on Oregon 224, the Upper Clackamas River Road, 26 miles to a junction just beyond Ripplebrook Campground. Keep right on Oregon 224 and several yards farther pass a sign indicating the mileage to Bagby Hot Springs. After 3.6 miles keep right on S-63, cross the Clackamas River and continue 3.0 miles on S-63 to the junction of S-70. Turn right onto S-70 and proceed 5.0 miles to Pegleg Campground. Continue on the main road 0.5 mile farther, turn left into a large parking area where a sign near the southwest edge marks the beginning of the hike.

Several yards along the trail cross a bridge and walk near a large stream for a few hundred feet then begin climbing gradually through a scenic forest of vine maple and widely spaced conifers. A section of trail along a poorly drained area has been reconstructed with planks to provide a better tread. Traverse above the stream then veer away from the flow and come to a long, narrow footbridge. Few hikers can resist stopping along the span to peer down into the several pools.

At the east end of the bridge curve right and climb a short distance. An unsigned trail that heads uphill to your left originally went to Pansy Basin (No. 56) but now the route ends in a clearcut. Just beyond this junction cross a small footbridge and climb the final 0.1 mile to the Bagby Guard Station. The bathhouse is down the slope to the north of the station. The Springs were named for Robert W. Bagby, a prospector and miner who once worked the area.

Bridge over Hot Springs Fork

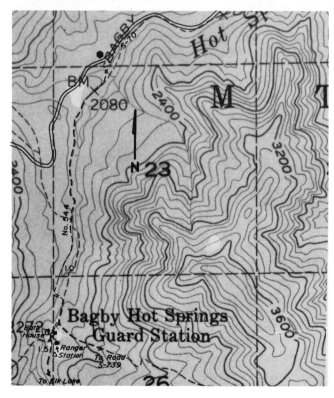

56 PANSY BASIN and BULL of the WOODS

One day trip or backpack
Distance: 3.6 miles one way
Elevation gain: 2,150 feet
High point: 5,523 feet
Allow 2 to 2½ hours one way
Usually open late June through mid-October
Topographic map:
  U.S.G.S. Battle Ax, Oreg.
  15'   1956

Although not enough above its neighbors to be easily identified from a distance, Bull of the Woods is high enough to provide a fine view of all the major Cascade Peaks from the Three Sisters north to Mt. Rainier, including Mt. Washington — which often can't be seen from summits in the Mt. Hood National Forest because Mt. Jefferson is in the way — and Three Fingered Jack. A few short portions of the climb are steep but, overall, the trail grade is moderate. You can make the return trip as a loop that involves no extra elevation gain and very little additional mileage.

Proceed southeast from Estacada on Oregon 224, the Upper Clackamas River Road, 26 miles to a junction just beyond Ripplebrook Campground. Continue to the right on Oregon 224 and 3.6 miles farther keep right on S-63 and after 5.5 miles turn right on S-708, leaving the paved surface for an oiled one. After 7.7 miles

keep right, following the sign pointing to Pansy Basin Trail, and 3.5 miles farther come to a sign on your left marking the beginning of the Pansy Basin Trail.

Walk through woods for a short distance then drop slightly into a sink hole. Cross the open area on a rocky trail then reenter deep woods. Climb gradually then more steeply before leveling off and descending briefly to a stream crossing at 0.8 mile. This is the last good source of water. Several yards beyond the flow come to the junction of the trail you'll be following if you make the loop.

Keep straight (right) and drop slightly into a meadow where an abundance of wildflowers bloom during mid-summer. Where the trail forks keep right and continue across the clearing. Near its west edge curve left and begin rising moderately through a rocky, semi-open area. Enter woods and begin climbing steeply then level off and pass near the east shore of a pond. Continue at a gradual grade to a shelter. Pansy Lake, not visible from the camp area, is about 100 feet downslope.

Continue along the trail that heads southwest from the shelter and begin climbing. Come to an open area at an old mine shaft where you can see down onto Pansy Lake and across upper Pansy Basin to the lookout tower on Bull of the Woods. Soon begin dropping and where a faint path heads south keep left on the main trail. Descend toward the lake for a short distance then curve sharply right and climb very steeply to a saddle at 1.9 miles and the junction of the Mother Lode Trail.

Turn left, traverse uphill and 0.3 mile from the saddle make a short set of switchbacks then continue traversing the wooded slope. Pass through a grassy patch and just below the ridge crest come to the junction of the trail to Welcome Lakes (No. 57). Turn left and traverse at a gradual grade for 0.3 mile then switchback right. After one more brief traverse make three short switchbacks and come to the summit area.

To make the loop, continue along the trail below the tower and descend to the north on the west side of the ridge. Enter woods and continue downhill along the crest before making two sets of switchbacks and crossing two grassy clearings. Go through a small burn and 1.0 mile from the lookout come to the junction of the trail past South and North Dickey Peaks. Turn left and continue dropping. Walk through an open area then pass above a large pond and wind down to the trail you followed on the way in.

Bull of the Woods lookout

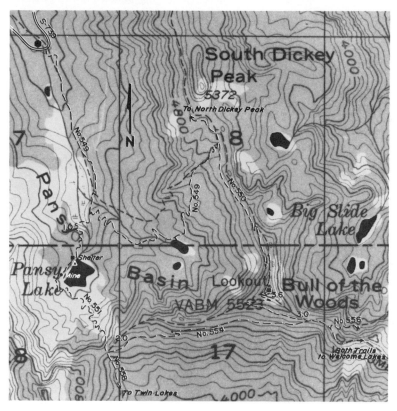

57 WELCOME LAKES

One day trip or backpack
Distance: 5 miles one way
Elevation gain: 2,000 feet; loss 200 feet
High point: 4,400 feet
Allow 2 hours one way
Usually open June through October
Topographic map:
** U.S.G.S. Battle Ax, Oreg.**
** 15'   1956**

The Welcome Lakes lie just east of Bull of the Woods (No. 56) and a visit to its summit where you can see the Cascade peaks from Three Sisters north to Mt. Rainier, is one of the several possible short side trips for day hikers and the network of trails in the area can keep a backpacker busy for days. The climb to Bull of the Woods and the little loop above West Lake on the return from the lookout would add a total of 4.0 miles and 1,600 feet of uphill.

Drive southeast from Estacada on Oregon 224, the Upper Clackamas River Road, 26 miles to a junction just beyond Ripplebrook Campground. Keep right on Oregon 224 and 3.6 miles farther veer right on Road S-63 and continue on it 14.7 miles to a bridge. Cross the span, keep right onto S-820 and proceed 0.5 mile to a clearcut and a sign stating Elk Lake Trail. Parking is available a few yards up the road.

After a few feet pass a sign listing several mileages and continue 0.2 mile through the clearcut to its western edge. Traverse along the sometimes rocky trail and resume climbing. Descend into the little side canyon formed by Pine Cone Creek, cross the flow and continue through woods. For the next mile red huckleberry bushes are abundant and the berries, that ripen in August, are delicious.

At 1.5 miles keep right at an old grey sign that marks the junction of the abandoned route to Janus Butte 1.5 miles to the south and travel at a gradual grade then descend to the crossing of Knob Rock Creek. Several feet farther ford a second stream, the last plentiful source of water along the hike, and climb to the junction of Trail No. 559 to Battle Creek Shelter and Elk Lake.

Stay right and begin a series of moderately steep switchbacks. The trail traverses a valley wall high above Welcome Creek and near 4.2 miles the grade becomes more gradual. Cross the base of a brush rimmed scree slope, hop a small stream and just beyond it pass an unmarked trail that descends to the lowest and largest of the Welcome Lakes.

The main trail climbs 0.2 mile to a large, dry campsite at the junction of the path to Upper Welcome Lake. Turn right and walk a few hundred feet to the lake that in late summer is covered with yellow pond lily blooms. From the viewpoint to the east of the lake you can look 200 feet down onto the lowest Welcome Lake.

To make the possible loops or to reach Bull of the Woods lookout return to the main trail and climb in short switchbacks through more open terrain to the junction of the Geronimo Trail. The route to the left goes to Elk Lake. Turn right onto No. 554 and travel near the crest to the Schreiner Peak Trail. To reach Bull of the Woods keep left, continue near the crest for 0.8 mile then keep right at the next junction and continue the final 0.4 mile up to the summit.

To make the return loop retrace your route from the lookout to the junction of the Schreiner Peak Trail, turn north and descend in very short, moderately steep switchbacks to the junction of the Dickey Creek Trail No. 553 to Big Slide Lake. Turn right, continuing on the Schreiner Peak Trail No. 555, and after a few yards pass a pond. Cross a saddle and come to the junction of West Lake Way. Turn right and descend gradually, traversing 250 feet above West Lake. Round a corner, descend to the northeastern shore of Upper Welcome Lake and continue the few hundred feet to the main trail, No. 554.

Lower Welcome Lake

58 AVERILL LAKE

One day trip or backpack
Distance: 3.8 miles one way
Elevation gain: 290 feet; loss 540 feet
High point: 5,240 feet
Allow 2 hours one way
Usually open late June through October
Topographic map:
  U.S.G.S. Breitenbush Lake, Oreg.
  15'   1961

The southeasternmost corner of the Mt. Hood National Forest supports an impressive number of lakes, large and small, and uncounted and unnamed ponds of various sizes. Three trails in this guide penetrate the heart of this area: Averill Lake, Fish Lake (No. 59) and Upper Lake (No. 61). Although not rugged, the terrain along the trek to Averill Lake is irregular enough that you occasionally have distant views, such as those of Mounts Jefferson and Hood and Olallie Butte (No. 60). Despite the proximity and profusion of lakes, carry drinking water as you'll be passing no fresh streams. Mosquitoes can be pests in the lake region during mid-summer.

Proceed southeast from Estacada on Oregon 224, the Upper Clackamas River Road, 48 miles to a sign identifying the way to Olallie Lake. Turn left onto Road S-806 and follow it 8.0 miles to the junction of the Skyline Road, S-42. The paved surface ends 0.1 mile before this intersection. Turn left onto S-42 and stay on it for 5.0 miles to the guard station and picnic area at the north end of Olallie Lake. Parking spaces are available off the east side of the road.

Since S-42 continues past Breitenbush Lake and rejoins FH 224, you also can approach the trailhead from the south. From the north end of the town of Detroit, turn northeast on FH 224 that is identified by a sign listing mileages to Breitenbush and Olallie Lakes. Follow FH 224 15.5 miles to the junction of S-42 at Round Pass (that may not be identified). Turn right onto the unpaved surface and drive 11 miles to the north end of Olallie Lake. You also can reach the junction of S-42 at Round Pass by following Oregon 224, that eventually becomes FH 224, 54 miles southeast from Estacada.

Cross S-42 from the picnic area and follow an old road that heads west for several yards then curve right and climb about 100 feet to the south end of Head Lake and a sign indicating the route to Upper Lake. Turn left and hike gradually uphill. Switchback once and travel above a pond covered with lily pads. Indians collected the ripened seeds from the yellow blooms and either toasted them or ground them into flour. Wind up and eventually have the first good view of Mt. Jefferson. Come to a small bench that holds an appropriately tiny tarn, curve left and begin traversing. You can see Twin Peaks nearby to the northwest and farther on you'll have a glimpse of Mt. Hood. Curve around the rocky south slope of Twin Peaks and climb gradually to the junction of two trails to Upper Lake.

If you want to make a short loop on your return, follow the trail to the left and descend 0.2 mile to Top Lake. Turn left and head east along Trail No. 719 for 0.9 mile to Road S-42 (see No. 61). You'll have to walk along the road for only 0.3 mile to reach your car.

To visit Averill Lake turn right onto Trail No. 719 at the four-way junction at 1.3 miles and climb a short distance then begin descending gradually. Pass a tarn below the rocky southwest slope of Twin Peaks and drop more noticeably along a rough tread to the junction of the trail to Lower Lake. This route, formerly part of the Pacific Crest Trail, meets the route to Fish Lake after 1.2 miles.

Turn left and walk on the level past small Fork Lake. Three-tenths mile farther come to Sheep Lake and the junction of the Potato Butte Trail that gains 450 feet in 1.0 mile to the summit of the cinder cone. Continue along the north shore of Sheep Lake and pass Wall Lake where you can see wooded Potato Butte just to the north. Drop slightly to large Averill Lake. The trail continues west 1.7 miles to Road S-46A.

Double Peaks from Averill Lake

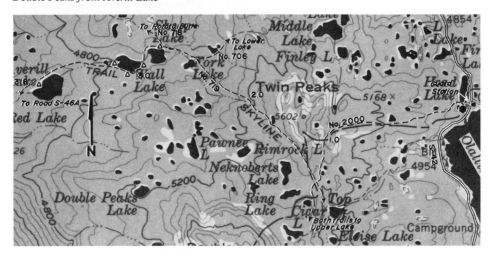

59 FISH LAKE

One-half day trip or backpack
Distance: 1.6 miles one way
Elevation loss: 550 feet
High point: 4,850 feet
Allow 45 minutes one way
Usually open late June through October
Topographic map:
  U.S.G.S. Breitenbush Lake, Oreg.
  15'   1961

Fish Lake is the second deepest in the Mt. Hood National Forest (Lost Lake just west of Mt. Hood is the deepest). The descent to it is the shortest of the three hikes (No's. 58 and 61 are the other two) in this mostly wooded area of uncounted lakes and tarns. From the junction at 0.8 mile you could head northeast toward Olallie Meadows or south into the heart of the lake country. Or, if you wanted to establish a car shuttle, you could make a scenic 7.3 mile traverse south to Breitenbush Lake. Combine No's. 58, 61 and 62 for a description of this trip.

Drive southeast from Estacada on Oregon 224, the Upper Clackamas River Road, 48 miles to a sign identifying the way to Olallie Lake. Turn left onto Road S-806 and follow it 8.0 miles to the junction of the Skyline Road, S-42. The paved surface ends 0.1 mile before this intersection. Turn right onto S-42 and stay on it for 4.1 miles to the entrance to Lower Lake Campground. Drive to the west (far) end of the campground where a sign marks the beginning of the Fish Lake Trail.

Since S-42 continues past Breintenbush Lake and rejoins FH 224, you also can approach the trailhead from the south. From the north end of the town of Detroit, turn northeast on FH 224 that is identified by a sign listing mileages to Breitenbush and Olallie Lakes. Follow FH 224 15.5 miles to the junction of S-42 at Round Pass (that may not be identified). Turn right onto the unpaved surface, drive 11 miles to the north end of Olallie Lake and continue 0.9 mile farther to Lower Lake Campground. You also can reach the junction of S-42 at Round Pass by following Oregon 224, that eventually becomes FH 224, 54 miles southeast from Estacada.

Walk almost on the level then begin descending and come to large Lower Lake. Contour along the northeastern shore and just beyond its end come to the junction of Trail No. 706 that heads south through the lake country and northeast toward Olallie Meadow beside S-42. Trail No. 706 used to be the route of the Pacific Crest Trail but recently it was rerouted to cross S-42 at the north end of Olallie Lake. If you head south along No. 706, after 1.2 miles you'll come to the junction of the Averill Lake Trail (No. 58) and 1.4 miles farther you'll meet the new section of the Pacific Crest Trail above Top Lake (see No. 61).

To reach Fish Lake keep straight on No. 717 and continue down through deeper woods. Pass an overlook several feet off the trail where you can see down onto the lake. Wind down in four switchbacks, cross the inlet creek, the only source of water along the hike, and continue to the shore.

The trail travels near the west shore, goes under power lines — the same ones you park near at the beginning of the climb to Olallie Butte (No. 60) — and continues a short distance past Si Lake to Road S-829A.

Fish Lake

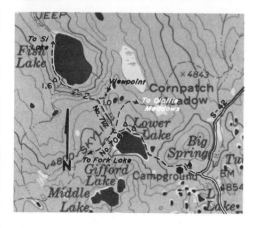

60 OLALLIE BUTTE

One day trip
Distance: 4 miles one way
Elevation gain: 2,575 feet
High point: 7,215 feet
Allow 2 to 2½ hours one way
Usually open mid-July through October
Topographic map:
  U.S.G.S. Breitenbush Hot Springs, Oreg.
  15'   1961

Olallie Butte is the large rounded peak just 10 miles north of Mt. Jefferson on the eastern rim of the High Cascades and is an easily identified landmark from many highpoints in the Mt. Hood National Forest and elsewhere. The hike to the summit is along a smooth, moderately graded trail and at the top you'll have ap-propriately far-ranging view that extends north to Mounts St. Helens, Rainier and Adams, south to the Three Sisters, west over the wood-ed slopes of the Cascades and east across the fields of central Oregon. Carry water as none is available along the route.

Proceed southeast from Estacada on Oregon 224, the Upper Clackamas River Road, 48 miles to a sign identifying the way to Olallie Lake. Turn left onto Road S-806 and follow it 8.0 miles to the junction of the Skyline Road, S-42. The paved surface ends 0.1 mile before this in-tersection. Turn right onto S-42 and take it 3.0 miles to a sign on your left under the power lines marking the beginning of the Olallie Butte Trail No. 720. Parking is available just beyond the trailhead off the right (west) side of the road.

Since Road 224 continues to the community of Detroit, you also can approach from the south. From the north end of Detroit turn northeast on FH 224 that is identified by a sign listing mileages to Breitenbush, Elk and Olallie Lakes. Follow FH 224, that eventually becomes Oregon 224, 21.5 miles to the junction of S-806, turn right and proceed as described above.

Hike gradually uphill near the power lines for 200 yards to the junction of the Pacific Crest Trail. The section to the southwest passes Olallie Lake after 2.0 miles (see No. 58) and the route northeast reaches Jude Lake in 1.5 miles.

Keep straight on Trail No. 720 and soon begin climbing. You'll be able to glimpse the summit area a few times as you wind up the wooded slope. Beyond the midway point the trees become shorter and thicker and the groundcover is sparse.

Have your first views of the major peaks to the north then near 3.0 miles begin a long traverse to the southwest along an open slope. Enter woods of weathered trees then make seven switchbacks to the large summit area. During this final climb you'll have views over Olallie Lake and down onto a cluster of con-siderably smaller ones.

To reach the rubble of the cupola style lookout cabin that once stood on the summit, turn left at the crest and walk a short distance. This charming design once graced the tops of many highpoints in the Cascades but with the collapse of the one on Olallie Butte, none re-main. Before you begin the descent, head south along the crest from the junction to the other end of the summit ridge where you can look down on the menacing rock formations that protrude from the steeper east side. These are plugs of lava that have thus far resisted erosion.

Mt. Jefferson from Olallie Butte

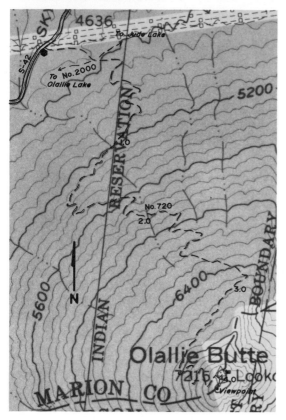

61 UPPER LAKE

One day trip or backpack
Distance: 1.7 miles one way
Elevation gain: 450 feet; loss 100 feet
High point: 5,400 feet
Allow 1½ hours one way
Usually open late June through October
Topographic map:
U.S.G.S. Breitenbush Lake, Oreg.
15'   1961

Upper Lake is the most southerly of the uncounted lakes and tarns in this corner of the Mt. Hood National Forest. If you want a longer hike you have the opportunity to make several side trips: a mile long path near the beginning goes to Timber Lake; you could continue south beyond Upper Lake and the Pacific Crest Trail to Ruddy Hill (No. 62) or set up a car shuttle and hike farther south to Breitenbush Lake; or you could head north to Averill (No. 58) or Fish (No. 59) Lakes; a little loop is possible midway along the trail to Upper Lake and one also can be made near the end by returning along the Pacific Crest Trail to Road S-42 (see No. 58). Regardless of the routes you follow, however, carry water because, despite

the impressive number of lakes and tarns, there are no streams.

Drive southeast from Estacada on Oregon 224, the Upper Clackamas River Road, 48 miles to a sign identifying the way to Olallie Lake. Turn left onto Road S-806 and follow it 8.0 miles to the junction of the Skyline Road, S-42. The paved surface ends 0.1 mile before this intersection. Turn right onto S-42 and stay on it for 5.0 miles to the guard station at the north end of Olallie Lake. Continue along S-42 0.3 mile more to a small sign off the west side of the road pointing to Top and Breitenbush Lakes. A few parking spaces are available off the east shoulder.

Since S-42 continues past Breitenbush Lake and rejoins FH 224, you also can approach the trailhead from the south. From the north end of the community of Detroit turn northeast on FH 224 that is identified by a sign listing mileages to Breitenbush and Olallie Lakes. Follow FH 224 15.5 miles to the junction of S-42 at Round Pass (that may not be signed). Turn right onto the unpaved surface and proceed 10.7 miles to the trailhead. You also can reach Round Pass by following Oregon 224, that eventually becomes FH 224, 54 miles southeast from Estacada.

Climb for a short distance then travel on the level through open terrain of scattered trees past several tarns. Resume hiking uphill, passing more tarns, and descend briefly to the junction of the trail to Timber Lake. Keep straight and climb gradually uphill 0.2 mile to Top Lake. Beyond its west end come to the junction of the Pacific Crest Trail No. 2000. If you plan to make the short loop on the return, take the trail to the right and climb 0.2 mile to a junction. Trail No. 719 continues northwest from here to Averill Lake. Turn right, staying on No. 2000, descend to S-42 and follow it south 0.3 mile to your starting point.

To continue the hike to Upper Lake, turn left onto No. 2000 at Top Lake and walk south. Enter deeper woods and climb in three switchbacks then at the fourth turn come to the junction of a trail that heads north and rejoins the Pacific Crest Trail at the junction 0.2 mile above Top Lake.

Turn left and immediately pass Cigar Lake. Walk through a more open area that is dotted with tarns. During this final portion you'll have views of Mt. Jefferson. Come to the northeast end of Upper Lake just before the resumption of the dense timber. Trail No. 2000 continues south and passes the 0.3 mile spur to Ruddy Hill (No. 62) after 1.5 miles.

Upper Lake

62 RUDDY HILL LOOP

One day trip
Distance: 4 miles round trip
Elevation gain: 1,000 feet round trip
High point: 5,943 feet
Allow 3 hours round trip
Usually open July through October
Topographic map:
  U.S.G.S. Breitenbush Lake, Oreg.
  15'   1961

The Ruddy Hill loop that begins near Breitenbush Lake is an interesting trip with a variety of scenery and views that extend north to Mt. St. Helens, south to Mt. Jefferson just 6.5 miles away and down onto Olallie, Horseshoe and Breitenbush Lakes. If you want a longer trip you could continue north along the Pacific Crest Trail from the junction at 1.7 miles to Upper Lake (No. 61). Carry water as there are no streams along the hike. A car shuttle could be established but the walk along Road S-42 between the start and finish of the loop is only 0.6 mile.

Proceed southeast from Estacada on Oregon 224, the Upper Clackamas River Road (that eventually becomes FH 224), 54 miles to the junction of S-42 at Round Pass (that may be unsigned). Turn left onto unpaved S-42 and follow it 7.4 miles to a sign on your left stating Gibson Lake Trail. This is 0.5 mile beyond the entrance to the campground at Breitenbush Lake and you could leave your car here. You also can reach S-42 from Detroit. At the south end of the community turn northeast onto FH 224 as indicated by a sign listing mileages to Breitenbush and other lakes and follow it 15.5 miles to the junction of S-42.

Traverse uphill then curve left and walk on the level along the edge of a plateau. Pass a tarn on your right then come to Gibson Lake and travel around its north shore where you'll have a nicely framed view of Mt. Jefferson.

Begin traversing gradually uphill along an open slope. Horseshoe Lake is directly below, Olallie Lake is just beyond it and Olallie Butte (No. 60) and Mounts Hood and St. Helens are the high points to the north. Descend into denser woods then resume traveling in the open where you can see Ruddy Hill. You may miss the junction of Trail No. 2000, at 1.6 miles, that you'll be taking back to S-42 but the fork is obvious when you're returning to the south. Drop through deep woods to the junction of the Horseshoe Saddle Trail No. 712. Keep left and continue several hundred yards along No. 2000 to a sign stating *Ruddy Hill ½*. The Pacific Crest Trail continues on the level through woods for 1.5 miles to Upper Lake.

Keep left and climb very steeply for 0.2 mile to the crest of the ridge. Turn left and continue up at a more moderate angle for 0.1 mile to the summit. The nearby north face of Mt. Jefferson is the most fascinating and conspicuous feature but if you're familiar with the north central Cascades, you'll be able to identify many landmarks to the southwest, such as Bachelor Mountain.

To make the return loop retrace your route to the junction at 1.6 miles and keep right on No. 2000, as indicated by the sign pointing to Breitenbush Lake. Climb gradually and briefly travel just several yards above the trail you followed in. Continue up then traverse a rocky slope where you'll have another fine view of Mt. Jefferson. Walk across a little bowl and go around the north shore of a large tarn. Continue on the level between two more tarns then have a glimpse of Breitenbush Lake just before beginning the 0.2 mile descent to Road S-42. Turn left and walk up the road to your car.

Tarn along trail

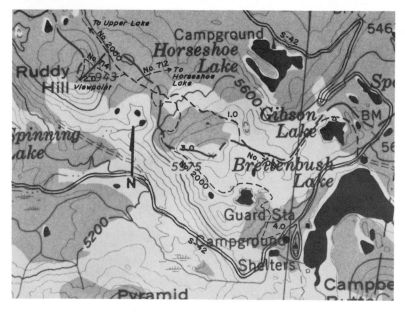

alphabetical index of trails

Editor: Thomas K. Worcester
Cover photo: Mt. Hood from near Cairn Basin